ADULT CLASS MANUAL

Adult Class Manual

For Adults Preparing for Baptism
or Confirmation

By
MARTIN ANDERSON, D. D.

AMBASSADOR PUBLICATIONS
Minneapolis, Minnesota

This limited edition licensed by
special permission of Augsburg Fortress.

The Board of Parish Education
The Association of Free Lutheran Congregations
3110 East Medicine Lake Boulevard
Minneapolis, Minnesota 55441.

2004 – 3000 copies

FOREWORD

Lutheran pastors are frequently given the privilege of instructing adults in preparation for baptism or confirmation. The scarcity or total absence in our church of suitable handbooks of instruction for such classes has led to the publication of this manual. Rev. Martin Anderson, the author, has had years of experience in the instruction of adult catechumens. It came to the attention of the Board that in doing this work Dr. Anderson had gathered some material suitable for such instruction. The Board thereupon asked Dr. Anderson to prepare an adult class manual. This he has done with results which the Board feels are very gratifying. The Board has considered and reviewed each lesson and sends forth this little handbook confident that it will fill a real want and with the prayer that God will bless it in bringing to those who use it a deeper knowledge of God's way of salvation through faith which is in Jesus Christ as revealed in the Word of God and taught in the Lutheran Church.

THE BOARD OF CHRISTIAN EDUCATION

PREFACE

The purpose of this little volume is to provide a book of instruction for adults who desire to join the Lutheran Church through baptism or confirmation.

It has fallen to the lot of the writer to instruct several groups of adults who either were not baptized, or, being baptized, were not confirmed. There was always the problem — what textbook, or treatise, should be put into the hands of these people? Several books have been used all of which have some merit. But none of them were quite satisfactory since they had not really been prepared specifically for this use. Upon inquiry among other pastors, the writer has found that others have experienced the same difficulty. The present volume is written for the specific purpose stated in the first paragraph of this preface. It has grown out of the author's experience with such adult classes. How far this handbook is any improvement on material already available is for others to say.

The division of the subject matter into ten chapters contemplates ten lessons or meetings with the individual or group. The folks with whom one has to deal in these classes are generally busy people. Often there are among them mothers of little children. Some may have night work, while others have day work. The matter of arranging a time when all members of the class can meet is often difficult, hence it may be necessary to reduce the number of meetings. Five ought to be the minimum. If it can be arranged to have the baptismal or confirmation service at the regular hour of public worship, this is in many ways the best. Where this is not possible the service should still be held in the church, with officers of the church present. As a rule, it is advisable to administer the Lord's Supper at the same service.

It will be found that the members of these classes differ a great deal in their previous religious training and in their general educational equipment. They often come from several different denominations, Catholic and Reformed, as well as from no church. Some may have had considerable religious instruction and even have been Sunday school teachers; some may have had practically no religious training. Some may be college graduates, and some may have had extremely limited educational opportunities and may have been away from books and study for many years.

Obviously, it is not an easy task to prepare a manual that will be well adapted to the needs of all. The teacher in each case will have to supply as much explanation of the subject matter as the circumstances may require.

Opinions will differ as to the amount of memory work that should be required. The writer has contented himself with stating that all Christians should know the Ten Commandments, the Apostles' Creed, and, of course, the Lord's Prayer. Generally it will be found advisable to use the lecture method of instruction, with every encouragement to the class to ask questions. The Bible History may be assigned as collateral reading, or certain parts of the Bible, as for example one or more of the Gospels and the Epistle to the Galatians. The aim throughout all the instruction should be to prepare the heart as well as the head.

In preparing this volume, the author has received much help from the following works as well as others:

Norlie's *Open Bible*; Schmid's *Dogmatics*; Jacob's *Summary of the Christian Faith*; Stump's *Bible Teachings*; Gerberding's *Way of Salvation*; Garvic's *Handbook of Christian Truth*. The writer is also indebted for many valuable suggestions to the Board of Elementary Christian Education, under whose supervision this manual is written.

This *Adult Class Manual* has been prepared with the prayer that under God it may help inquirers after the truth to orientate themselves, and that it may warm their hearts through the precious truths of the Word of God, which are able to make men "wise unto salvation." May busy pastors also find this volume helpful in dealing with those for whose use it is intended.

MARTIN ANDERSON.

PREFACE TO THE REVISED EDITION

After fourteen printings of *The Adult Class Manual* this revised edition is sent forth. The changes in this edition are not many. Errors in the former edition, mainly in Scripture references, have been corrected. The chapter titles have been simplified. But the main change, which we trust is a definite improvement, is the addition of a set of questions at the end of each chapter. The obvious purpose is to focus the attention of the student on the most vital things in each chapter and to aid the teacher in securing the desired reactions from the student.

Our prayer is that by the blessing of God this little volume may continue to be helpful to seekers after truth and to the pastors who instruct them.

MARTIN ANDERSON.

Chicago, Illinois, March 10, 1938.

CONTENTS

CHAPTER ONE

THE BIBLE

The Bible (the canonical books of the Old and New Testaments) is the Word of God. It is a perfect and sufficient revelation of the will and works of the triune God, Father, Son, and Holy Spirit.

THE AUTHOR IS GOD

The author of the Bible is God. In giving His Word to us God used certain human writers, such as Moses, Isaiah, Matthew and Paul. But back of theses writers was God who so inspired or led them that what they wrote was the Word of God. "The Spirit of God revealed to them what they should say and write" (S.[1]4). "Holy men of God spake as they were moved by the Holy Spirit" (2 Peter 1:21). "All Scripture is given by inspiration of God" (2 Tim. 3:16).

The Bible thus is different from all other books in the world, because its source and authorship is different. This book is from God in an altogether different way from that of any other good book we might mention. It is inspired in the special sense that God chose these men for their work and revealed to them what they should say and write. Therefore, what they wrote

---

[1]The letter S. found in parenthesis here and elsewhere in this Manual, refers to Sverdrup's Explanation of Luther's Catechism. The number indicates the question.

is an infallible revelation of God. The Bible claims to be thus inspired (2 Peter 1:21; 2 Tim. 3:16; 2 Thess. 2:15; I Cor. 14:37; I Thess. 2:13), and this claim we must recognize and admit.

THE BIBLE IS THE SUPREME AUTHORITY

And because the Bible is inspired by God, it is the supreme authority in all matters of faith and life (The Norm). All doctrines as well as everything in our conduct must be tested by it and be in accord with it. Any doctrine that is not in full accord with the teachings of the Bible must be rejected. And anything in life and conduct which is contrary to the Bible is evil and must be opposed. The Bible is the supreme authority in all of these matters.

We find that Christ so many times asked, "What saith the Scriptures?" "Have ye not read?" "Is it not written?" The teachings of the Scriptures settled all matters for Him. Therefore when we are considering any question of doctrine, as, for example, the creation, the deity of Christ, the virgin birth of Christ, the purpose of Christ's suffering, or any other matter of religious belief, the only question is: "What does the Bible say?" Likewise in all questions of conduct, as, for example, our duties to our neighbor, the question of divorce, or the right observance of the Lord's Day, we have only to ascertain the teachings of the Bible on these points. We must say with our Lord, "What saith the Scriptures?" The Bible speaks the final word in all matters of faith and life.

The seat of authority is the Word of God. It is not human reason, for reason is not infallible. Reason often blunders. We are to use our reason to ascertain the meaning of Scripture, but not to judge of its merit. We cannot reject anything taught in the Word because it may not seem reasonable to us. We dare not be "wise above what is written."[2] Neither is conscience the seat of authority. Since the fall of man conscience has been unreliable. It often blunders. The apostle Paul acted according to his conscience when he persecuted the Christians. And the church is not the seat of authority, for the church is composed of fallible human beings.[3] Some might say, "Christ is the ultimate authority." But we find Him only in the Word. Hence we conclude that the ultimate seat of authority is the Word of God, the Bible.

The Bible does not need to be supplemented by tradition, by the decrees of councils or by human interpretations. We must neither add to it nor subtract from it. Any person of ordinary intelligence who will study the Bible without prejudice or preconceived notions as to what it ought to contain, and who will read with prayer for the enlightenment of the Holy Spirit, will find in the Bible what he needs to believe and do to be saved (2 Cor. 2:14). Each part of the Word is to be understood in the light shed upon it by all other parts. Thus the Bible becomes its own interpreter. The individual reader does not need to take anyone's word for what the Scriptures say. He has free access to the Word and under the guidance of the Holy Spirit he has the right of private judgment. We say, "Here is the open Bible, read it prayerfully and see for yourself just what it teaches."[4]

The Bible does not only *contain* the Word of God,

[2]Compare Reformed view.
[3]Compare Roman Catholic view.
[4]Compare Roman Catholic view.

but it *is* the Word of God. We cannot reduce it to the level of other books and sift out what we will believe, and reject the rest. Not all in the Bible is equally important, but nothing is unimportant. Every part is there for a purpose. All of it is the Word of God.

The right attitude to the Scriptures is to have this as our motto: *The Bible, the whole Bible, and nothing but the Bible.*

Nature of Contents
Proves Divine Authorship

There are many weighty reasons why we conclude that the Bible is the infallible revelation of God. We do not have to believe without proof. In the first place, the nature of the contents of the Bible is such that it proves it to be a divine revelation. Its teachings meet the needs of the human heart and answer satisfactorily the soul's deepest questions. Its history through many centuries shows that it has power to transform the lives of individuals and of nations. There is power in this book to change wholly the course of men's lives and to give their hearts peace. It takes hold of the heart as no other book. Man, unaided by divine inspiration, could no more have produced such a book than he could paint the sunset skies or make the rose. "The Bible contains knowledge which no man could have discovered by his own power. It foretells events which no uninspired man could have foreseen. It contains teachings so exalted and holy that they could not have originated in the heart of man. It possesses a power such as no merely human book ever did or could possess" (Stump's Explanation). "If any man will do His will, he shall know of the doctrine, whether it be of God" (John 7:17). If a man will believe and obey the teachings of the Bible and trust its promises he will find abundant proof in his own experience that this is not a mere human book. "He shall know of the doctrine, whether it be of God."

UNITY OF THE BIBLE
PROVES DIVINE AUTHORSHIP

The unity of the Bible also is a proof of its divine authorship. It is really a collection of books, sixty-six in all. There are about forty human authors. The several books were prepared over a period of about 1500 years. These writers lived in different countries and used different languages. They were mostly unknown to one another. The writers did not know the whole of which their several contributions were a part. Yet there is a perfect and wonderful unity of teaching and purpose, and perfect harmony throughout. The alleged contradictions are found upon examination to be only apparent. This unity of the Scriptures is further proof that the real author is God. The Bible is His inspired Word.

NATURE CORROBORATES THE BIBLE

The great world of nature points unmistakably to the truth of the Bible. "The heavens declare the glory of God; and the firmament showeth His handiwork" (Psalm 19:1). There is no conflict between the Bible and science. There are laws in nature. But God is the lawgiver. When there sometimes has seemed to be disagreement between the teachings of science and the teachings of the Bible, either the facts of nature have not been correctly ascertained, or the teachings of the Bible have not been rightly understood. Often unproved scientific theories are set forth as proved facts, and thus it is made to appear that there is a conflict between the Bible and science. The evidences of design in nature, of laws and forces that are ever at work, point to just such a Creator and Preserver of all things as the Bible makes known to us. Nature does not contradict the Bible; it corroborates the Bible.

THE POWER OF THE BIBLE TO SURVIVE

The power of the Bible to endure and survive all the attacks of its enemies also demonstrates its divine origin. "It is an anvil that has worn out many hammers." No book in the world has such a record. Men and devils have labored to destroy this book, but in vain. Men have argued against it, ridiculed it, ignored it. Still it lives. It is the world's best seller. It is mightier than all its foes and marches in triumph over the graves of its enemies. To quote F. Bettex in his, *The Bible the Word of God*: "The Bible, indeed not an ordinary book, hated and hounded as no other book ever has been; and yet indestructible; despised, and yet honored; derided, and yet highly esteemed; declared dead, and yet alive. Mighty emperors and kings and priests have shunned no toil and no guilt in order to exterminate it; wise and scholarly men have in the sweat of their brow thoroughly refuted it; and now that higher criticism lords over it and science has done away with it, it is spreading over the whole earth with astonishing rapidity in millions of copies and hundreds of languages, and is being read and preached from pole to pole; and in the faith and power of the Word, negroes submit to being burned alive, and Armenians and Chinese to being tortured to death. Ho, all ye scholars and critics, do but write such a book and we will believe you. Complete in itself — 'accursed any man that shall add unto or take away' — unchanged and unchangeable, this Bible stands for centuries, unconcerned about the praise and the reproach of men; it does not accommodate itself to progress, does not recant a single word, but remains grandly simple and divinely overpowering." "The Word of the Lord standeth sure." Surely a book with such a record and such a history is not a mere human document, but a divine revelation.

How firm a foundation, ye saints of the Lord,
Is laid for your faith in His excellent Word.

QUESTIONS
In what respect is the Bible different from all other books? In what sense is the Bible inspired? What is the final authority in all questions of doctrine and conduct? What is the place of reason in the study of the Bible? How does the nature of the contents of the Bible prove that the Bible is the Word of God? How does the unity of the books of the Bible prove that it is divinely inspired? Is there any conflict between the Bible and science?

CHAPTER TWO

GOD

The Bible makes God known to men. Even the heathen who do not have the Bible believe in some higher being to whom they feel accountable, who will punish their wrongdoing, and whose favor they seek. All men everywhere have a conscience which tells them that certain acts are wrong (Rom. 2:14-15).

Nature also, as mentioned in Chapter One, points clearly to a Creator and Preserver of all things (Rom. 1:19-20; S. 119). But only the Bible gives us a clear and complete revelation of our Maker. The central thought of the Bible is God. His name is on almost every page.

THE NATURE OF GOD

What is God? In this life we can never know God fully, nor adequately define Him. If we could, then we would be His equals and He would be no God. We can say, however, that God is an uncreated Spirit who is eternal, almighty, all-knowing, everywhere present, wise, good, merciful, holy, true and just (S. 120). (John 4:24, Ps. 90:2, Luke 1:37, 1 John 3:20, Acts 17:27, Ps. 104:24, I John 4:16, Ps. 106:1, Ps. 103:13, Is. 6:3, Numb. 23:19, Ps. 7:11.) God is a person, a personal being, without the limitations of human personality. God is not only a personification of the laws and forces at work in the universe (Pantheism). God is a personal being with infinite power, intelligence and love, who speaks to us and to whom we can speak. "God said, Let there be light: and there was light"

(Gen. 1:3). "And God spake all these words, saying, I am the Lord thy God, etc." (Exod. 20:1-2). Thus God, the great "I Am," speaks. And He bids us speak to Him and say, "Our Father who art in heaven." There are literally hundreds of passages in the Bible which are meaningless and absurd if we are not to believe that God is a person.[5] God is "a being holy and altogether righteous, hating sin — yet a being of infinite love and of tender mercy, loving the sinner and wooing the evil-doer with a tenderness and a constancy greater than that of a father or a mother."[6]

ONLY ONE GOD

The Bible teaches that there is only one God. "I am the Lord thy God, thou shalt have no other gods before me" (First Commandment). "Hear, O Israel: the Lord our God is one Lord" (Deut. 6:4). "There is one God" (1 Tim. 2:5). "God is one" (Gal. 3:20). There is but one only true God, and there is none else beside Him (S. 121).

THREE PERSONS

But while the Bible teaches that there is only one God, it also tells us that God is a Trinity; that there are three persons in God: the Father, the Son, and the Holy Spirit. "These three are one and perfectly equal to each other in nature and dignity" (S. 122). There is a profound mystery here which our finite reason can never fully understand. "The finite is unable to comprehend the infinite" (Stump, *Bible Teachings*). However, we must not reject this doctrine because we cannot fully grasp this idea. Every day and on every

[5]Compare Christian Science.
[6]Garvie's *Handbook of Christian Truth*.

hand we are confronted with things in nature which no man can understand. How then can we expect to fully comprehend God, who is the infinite and eternal Creator of the universe?

Though we cannot fully grasp the idea of the Trinity, it certainly is the teaching of Holy Writ. Each of the three persons is mentioned a great many times. Each was present at the baptism of Jesus (Matt. 3:13-17). The three persons are coordinated in the Apostolic Benediction (1 Cor. 1:3; 2 Cor. 1:2; Gal. 1:3; Eph. 1:2; Col. 1:2). We are commanded to baptize in the name of the Father, the Son and the Holy Spirit (Matt. 28:19). And to each of these persons is ascribed divine names, divine attributes, divine works, and divine worship. The Bible teaches that the Father is God. The Bible declares that the Son is true God. "The Word was God ... the Word became flesh and dwelt among us" (John 1:1). See further proof of the deity of Jesus Christ in Chapter Four. The Bible also declares that the Holy Spirit is true God. "Why hath Satan filled thine heart to lie to the Holy Spirit ... thou hast not lied unto men, but unto God" (Acts 5:3-4). See additional proof of the deity of the Holy Spirit in Chapter Six. The Bible thus clearly teaches that each of the persons of the Trinity is true God. And since we are also clearly taught that there is only one God, we conclude that in the one God there are three persons. There are not three Gods, but there are three persons in one being.

The three persons of the Godhead are equal in power and dignity, and not one above or below the other. They are placed side by side as equal. We recall Christ's command: "Go ye therefore, and make disciples of all the nations, baptizing them into the name of the Father and of the Son and of the Holy Spirit" (Matt. 28:19).

The Scriptures ascribe special works to each of the three persons, however, not exclusively but predominantly. The Father's special work is the creation, preservation. and government of the world; and He so loved the world that He gave His only begotten Son to become its Savior. The special work of the Son is redemption. He gave His life that we might live. The Holy Spirit's special work is sanctification. He works repentance and faith in the hearts of men. Yet all persons of the Trinity participate and cooperate in every divine act.

THE FATHER

The Father is the Creator and Preserver of the universe. He is the Great First Cause back of all that exists. He is the Father of Jesus Christ and He is our Father. In the First Article of the Apostles' Creed, the common confession of all Christians, we say:

"I believe in God the Father Almighty, Maker of heaven and earth."

Martin Luther has given us this explanation of the First Article:

I believe that God has made me and all creatures, that He has given and still preserves to me my body and soul, eyes, ears, and all my members, my reason and all my senses; also clothing and shoes, meat and drink, house and home, wife and child, land, cattle, and all my goods; that He richly and daily provides me with all that I need for this body and life, protects me against all danger, guards and keeps me from all evil; and all this purely out of fatherly divine goodness and mercy, without any merit or worthiness in me; for all which I am duty bound to thank and praise, serve and obey Him. This is most certainly true.

GOD AS CREATOR

The story of how God created the world is told in the first two chapters of the Bible, Gen. 1 and 2. "In the beginning God created the heavens and the earth" (Gen. 1:1). "In six successive days God (1) created the light and separated it from the darkness, (2) made the firmament, (3) divided the dry land from the sea and covered it with plant life, (4) set the sun, moon, and stars in their places, (5) made the fishes and the birds, (6) the beasts of the field, and finally man. On the seventh day God rested from His work and hallowed the day."[7] By His almighty word God brought forth the world and all that therein is. "He spake, and it was done; He commanded, and it stood fast" (Ps. 33:9). There is no materialistic philosophy of evolution that can make God superfluous or unnecessary as the Creator of the universe. On the contrary, the design seen everywhere in nature, and the laws of nature point unmistakably to such a Creator as the Bible reveals.

MAN CREATED

The climax of creation was man. "God created man in His own image, in the image of God created He him, male and female created He them" (Gen. 1:27). "And the Lord God formed man of the dust of the ground, and breathed into his nostrils the breath of life; and man became a living soul" (Gen. 2:7). In the beginning, man was endowed with perfect health and immortality. He lived a life free from care, pain, or distress of any kind. "He was without sin and like God." "In the

---

[7]Stump's *Bible Teachings*.

image of God created He him." "God saw every thing that He had made, and, behold, it was very good" (Gen. 1:31).

That which more than anything else makes man different from the rest of creation is his moral sense. Man is a moral being. Even in the midst of heathendom he is more or less concerned about the rightness or wrongness of his acts. Man, therefore, cannot be "the product of a blind, unintelligent, non-moral force."[8] That which is in the effect must be in the cause. And as man is a moral spirit he must have sprung from some great moral Being whose nature he shares. The nature of man points clearly to Jehovah, the God of revelation, as his Creator.

GOD AS PRESERVER

God is not only our Creator; He is also our Preserver. He is the Almighty. But He is not a powerful despot, ruling the universe with an iron scepter. He is our Father, who ever seeks the good of His children. We can confidently resign all our affairs into His hands, knowing that He will watch over us and care for us. "Casting all your care upon Him; for He careth for you" (I Peter 5:7). We are wholly dependent upon Him. "In Him we live, and move, and have our being" (Acts 17:28). "He giveth to all life and breath and all things" (Acts 17:25). He must send rain and sunshine in right proportions, so that the harvests may yield plentifully and the granaries may be filled. "The eyes of all wait upon Thee and Thou givest them their meat in due season. Thou openest Thine hand, and satisfi-

---

[8]Garvic's *Handbook of Christian Truth*.

est the desire of every living thing" (Ps. 145:15-16).
"Therefore I say unto you, Take no thought for your
life, what ye shall eat, or what ye shall drink; nor yet
for your body, what ye shall put on. Is not the life
more than meat, and the body than raiment? ...
Wherefore, if God so clothe the grass of the field,
which today is, and tomorrow is cast into the oven,
shall He not much more clothe you, O ye of little faith?
Therefore take no thought, saying, What shall we eat?
or, What shall we drink? or, Wherewithal shall we be
clothed? ... for your heavenly Father knoweth that ye
have need of all these things. But seek ye first the
kingdom of God, and His righteousness; and all these
things shall be added unto you" (Matt. 6:25, 30-33.
See also Ps. 121). "All this He does purely out of
fatherly divine goodness and mercy without any merit
or worthiness in me; for all which I am in duty bound
to thank and praise, to serve and obey Him."

QUESTIONS

Give some Scripture passages which teach that
there is only one God. Give some passages which
teach that there are three persons in the Godhead.
What special work is ascribed to the Father? To the
Son? To the Holy Spirit? What was the state of man as
God created him? How does Luther's explanation of
the First Article describe the Heavenly Father's loving
care?

CHAPTER THREE

SIN

When God created Adam and Eve, He did not make two sinners. Man in the beginning was a perfect being. "God created man in His own image, in the image of God created He him" (Gen.1:21).

THE FALL

God put a test of obedience in the garden of Eden.

"And the Lord God commanded the man, saying, Of every tree of the garden thou mayest freely eat: but of the tree of knowledge of good and evil, thou shalt not eat of it: for in the day that thou eatest thereof thou shalt surely die" (Gen. 2:16-17). Man was given a free will. He could choose between obedience and disobedience. The devil came to Eve in the form of a serpent and tempted her to eat of the forbidden fruit. She yielded to the temptation and ate of the fruit. Adam also disobeyed God and ate of this tree. And God expelled Adam and Eve from the beautiful garden of Eden. Thus man fell from the state of innocence and happiness and became a sinful and lost being. This is called the Fall of Man (See Genesis, Chapter 3).

The result of the Fall was that man became unfit to live in communion and fellowship with God. He deserved God's wrath and eternal exclusion from Him. Death entered into the world. Man's body became mortal. Sin brought upon it sickness and suffering with death in the end. Man lost his life in God (spiritual life). He became spiritually dead. His mind became darkened in spiritual matters, and he lost his free will in spiritual things. His will became inclined to evil, but powerless to do good. By his own power man can do only evil as a result of the Fall. Thus God fulfilled His threat. "In the day that thou eatest thereof thou shalt surely die" (Gen. 2:17). "The wages of sin is death" (Rom. 6:23). "The carnal mind is enmity against God: for it is not subject to the law of God, neither indeed can be" (Rom. 8:7).

ALL ARE BORN SINNERS

"After Adam's Fall, all men begotten according to the common course of nature are born with sin" (Augsburg Confession). Sin and its result, death, have been transmitted from our first parents to the whole human race. Every child is born with the taint of sin upon it, and with a nature that inclines it to sin. We have an inherited inclination to evil. The babe that is just born is not like Adam and Eve as God created them. This babe has the seeds and roots of sin in its nature. It will be *natural* for it to sin. This child is spiritually dead until it is raised to life (regeneration) by the grace of God. This is the plain teaching of the Bible. "Behold, I was shapen in iniquity; and in sin did my mother conceive me" (Ps. 51:5). "That which is born of the flesh is flesh" (John 6). (See John 3:3-16.) We "were by nature the children of wrath" (Eph. 2:3); "By one man sin entered into the world, and death by sin; and so death passed upon all men, for that all have sinned" (Rom. 5:12).

But we have not only these passages of the Word of God to tell us that every child is born with a sinful heart, that inclines it to evil. Our own observation and reason tell us the same. We know that we do not have to teach a child to be selfish, angry, jealous, self-willed, or stubborn. More or less of this is natural for every child. The child is only following its natural bent when it manifests any of these sinful traits. On the other hand, we have to teach a child to be truthful, unselfish, not to give pain to others, and similar good traits of character. Thus we learn from observation, as well as from Scripture, that the corruption of sin is upon us from birth. We are born sinners. Even the newborn babe needs God's grace.

All are born sinners, and none of us can keep the law of God perfectly. "There is not a just man upon earth, that doeth good, and sinneth not" (Eccl. 7:20). Some are worse than others, but "There is none righteous, no, not one" (Rom. 3:10). All have broken God's commands countless times. "If we say that we have no sin, we deceive ourselves, and the truth is not in us. ... If we say that we have not sinned, we make Him a liar, and His word is not in us (I John 1:8, 10). The best person on earth is still only a sinner, as he will realize when he attempts to keep the law.

GOD'S LAW ACCUSES US

The law of God reveals our sins. "By the law is the knowledge of sin" (Rom. 3:20). The law is like a looking glass that shows us all the smirch and flaws. This law is contained in the Ten Commandments which God Himself gave to Moses on Mount Sinai.

THE TEN COMMANDMENTS[9]

THE FIRST COMMANDMENT

I am the Lord thy God.

Thou shalt have no other gods before me.

What is meant by this?

We should fear, love, and trust in God above all things.

THE SECOND COMMANDMENT

Thou shalt not take the name of the Lord thy God in vain; for the Lord will not hold him guiltless that taketh His name in vain.

What is meant by this?

We should fear and love God, and not curse, swear, conjure, lie or deceive by His name, but call upon the same in every need, and worship Him with prayer, praise and thanksgiving.

THE THIRD COMMANDMENT

Remember the sabbath day to keep it holy.

What is meant by this?

We should fear and love God, and not despise preaching and His Word, but deem it holy and gladly hear and learn it.

THE FOURTH COMMANDMENT

Honor thy father and thy mother, that it may be well with thee, and thou mayest live long upon the earth.

What is meant by this?

We should fear and love God, and not despise our parents and superiors, nor provoke them to anger, but honor, serve, obey, love and esteem them.

THE FIFTH COMMANDMENT

Thou shalt not kill.

---

[9]Quoted from Luther's Catechism.

What is meant by this?

We should fear and love God, and not hurt nor harm our neighbor in his body, but help and befriend him in every bodily need.

THE SIXTH COMMANDMENT

Thou shalt not commit adultery.

What is meant by this?

We should fear and love God, and be chaste and pure in words and deeds, each one loving and honoring his spouse.

THE SEVENTH COMMANDMENT

Thou shalt not steal.

What is meant by this?

We should fear and love God, and not take our neighbor's money or property, nor get it by false or unfair dealing, but help to improve and protect his property and living.

THE EIGHTH COMMANDMENT

Thou shalt not bear false witness against thy neighbor.

What is meant by this?

We should fear and love God, and not belie, betray, slander, nor defame our neighbor, but excuse him, speak well of him, and put the best construction on all he does.

THE NINTH COMMANDMENT

Thou shalt not covet thy neighbor's house.

What is meant by this?

We should fear and love God, and not desire to gain craftily our neighbor's inheritance or home, nor to get it by a show of right, but help and serve him in keeping it.

THE TENTH COMMANDMENT

Thou shalt not covet thy neighbor's wife, nor his manservant, nor his maidservant, nor his cattle, nor anything that is his.

What is meant by this?

We should fear and love God, and not estrange force, or entice away from our neighbor, his wife, servants, cattle, but urge them to stay and do their duty.

What does God say of all these commandments?

He says: I the Lord thy God am a jealous God, visiting the iniquity of the fathers upon the children unto the third and fourth generation of them that hate me; and showing mercy unto thousands of them that love me and keep my commandments.

What is meant by this?

God threatens to punish all who transgress these commandments; therefore we should fear His wrath, and do nothing against them. But He promises grace and every blessing to all who keep them; therefore we should love and trust in Him, and gladly do according to His commandments.

These commandments must be kept in the heart, not only outwardly. It is to the heart God says, "Thou shalt not kill," and "Thou shalt not steal," and so with all the commandments. Sin is every transgression of the law of God, whether in thought, word, or deed. The law demands the whole man. "Thou shalt love the Lord thy God with all thy heart, and with all thy soul, and with all thy strength, and with all thy mind" (Luke 10:27). It requires a perfect unselfishness. "Thou shalt love thy neighbor as thyself" (Matt. 22:39). Moreover, sins of omission are as grievous as sins of commission. "To him that knoweth to do good, and doeth it not, to him it is sin" (James 4:17). See also Matt. 25:42-46, "I was an hungered, and ye gave me no meat ..." Sometimes we sin without realizing it. "Who can understand his errors? Cleanse Thou me from secret faults" (Ps. 19:12). But here, as in civil affairs, ignorance of the law excuses no one. "The good that I would do I do not: but the evil which I would not, that I do" (Rom. 7:19). This is our common experience. We are compelled to reach this conclusion: *Before the bar of Almighty God, no man can plead "not guilty."*

Thus, without the grace of God, man is a poor, lost and condemned creature. He has broken God's law and offended against a kind and righteous Father, who is his Maker and Preserver. And while God is good and merciful, He also hates sin and abhors it. His holiness and justice are as infinite as His love. Man deserves His wrath and eternal separation from Him. Man needs forgiveness, cleansing, and power. What shall he do to be saved?

QUESTIONS

What test of man's obedience did God place in the Garden of Eden? What was the result of man's fall? What is the meaning of "we are by nature the children of wrath"? (Eph. 2:3.) What is the meaning of "by the law is the knowledge of sin"? (Rom. 3:20.) What have we deserved by reason of our sin?

CHAPTER FOUR

THE SAVIOR

God looked down upon sinful man and pitied him because of the misery which he had brought upon himself, and He yearned to help him. The love of God sought to find a way whereby all men could be saved. God would not leave the sinner in the dark. In His love He has made it possible for the sinner to return to the fold of his heavenly Father. *"God so loved the world that He gave His only begotten Son, that whosoever believeth in Him should not perish, but have everlasting life"* (John 3:16).

THE SECOND ARTICLE[10]
OF REDEMPTION

I believe in Jesus Christ, His only Son, our Lord; who was conceived by the Holy Ghost, born of the Virgin Mary, suffered under Pontius Pilate, was crucified, dead, and buried; He descended into hell; the third day He rose from the dead; He ascended into heaven, and sitteth on the right hand of God the Father Almighty; from thence He shall come to judge the quick and the dead.

What does this mean?

I believe that Jesus Christ, true God, begotten of the Father from eternity, and also true man, born of the Virgin Mary, is my Lord; who has redeemed me, a lost and condemned creature, purchased and won me from all sin, from death and the power of the devil, not with gold and silver, but with His holy precious blood, and with His innocent sufferings and death; in order that I might be His own, live under Him in His kingdom, and serve Him in everlasting righteousness, innocence and blessedness, even as He is

---

[10]Quoted from Luther's Catechism.

risen from the dead, lives and reigns to all eternity. This is most certainly true.

Thus the love of God has prepared a way for man's salvation.

How could God be a just and holy God and still save sinful men who had rebelled against His authority? We must remember that God's justice and His holiness are as infinite as His love. In the way of salvation to be provided the demands of justice must be satisfied. Justice demanded that sin be punished and that God's law be kept.

God's wisdom and love found the solution. *God Himself, in man's stead, would fulfill the law and suffer the punishment of sin in the person of His Son, Jesus Christ.* Thus, "Mercy and truth are met together; righteousness and peace have kissed each other" (Ps. 85:10). "God was in Christ, reconciling the world unto Himself" (2Cor 5:19). "O the depth of the riches both of the wisdom and knowledge of God! How unsearchable are His judgments, and His ways past finding out" (Rom. 11:33). Infinite love reaches down to lift men up again. God in Christ goes down into the pit, at a terrible cost to Himself, that man might be restored to God's favor and fellowship once more. "Not man, but God conceived and carried into execution the way of man's return" (Garvie).

God purposed from eternity to save us. On the very day man yielded to the tempter, the first promise of the Savior was given. Eve was led astray by the devil. But a descendant of Eve should come to destroy the work of the devil, at the cost, however, of His own suffering. "I will put enmity between thee and the woman, and between thy seed and her seed; *it shall bruise thy head, and thou shalt bruise his heel*[11] (Gen. 3:15). The promise of the coming Savior (Messiah) was repeated from time to time down through the ages. To Abraham, Isaac, Jacob, and David, the promise was given, until "when the fullness of the time was come, God sent forth His Son, made of a woman, made under the law" (Gal. 4:4). Mary, Joseph's betrothed, is honored above all the women of the world, and becomes the mother of our Redeemer. On that first wonderful Christmas night an angel announced to shepherds who were watching their sheep on the plains of Bethlehem that the Lord was come. "Unto you is born this day in the city of David a Savior, who is Christ the Lord" (Luke 2:11). And a multitude of the heavenly host praised God, saying, "Glory to God in the highest, and on earth peace, good will toward men" (Luke 2:14).

SALVATION PROVIDED FOR ALL

God's plan of salvation includes all men. "Behold I bring you good tidings of great joy, which shall be to all people" (Luke 2:10). "So God loved the *world*" (John 3:16). "Who will have all men to be saved, to come unto the knowledge of the truth" (1 Tim. 2:4). "As I live, saith the Lord God, I have no pleasure in the death of the wicked; but that the wicked turn from his way and live" (Ezek. 33:11). Christ is for every race and every generation and every individual. "He is the propitiation for our sins: and not for ours only, but also for the sins of the whole world" (1 John 2:2). The

---

[11]The italics in Bible verses throughout the book are the author's.

love of God in Christ is the red thread that runs through the whole Bible. The summary of all the books of the Bible "is the great truth that Jesus is the way of salvation for all believing souls" (S.9). To take Christ out of the Bible would be like taking the sun out of the solar system. In Christ God's love has done its utmost. He is the all-sufficient Savior of the world. "How shall we escape, if we neglect so great salvation?" (Heb. 2:3.) If we reject this Savior there is no other. He is the only star of hope for sinful men.

TRUE MAN AND TRUE GOD

Concerning the *person* of the Savior, the Bible teaches that He was both *human* and *divine*. He is God and man in one person. He is the God-Man.

Jesus Christ was "true man, born of the Virgin Mary" (Second Article). He had a body like ours, and He was subject to hunger, thirst, and fatigue, just as we are. He needed to eat and drink and rest and care for His body, just like other men. He could be tempted and He could die. He was "true man." "There is one God and one mediator between God and men, the *man* Christ Jesus" (1 Tim. 2:5). "The Word was made flesh, and dwelt among us" (John 1:14; Heb. 2:17).

But He was not only a man. "He is true God, begotten of the Father from eternity" (Second Article). The Bible ascribes to Him divine names, divine attributes, divine works, and divine worship. There is need of emphasizing this because Unitarians, Universalists, and many in other denominations deny the deity of Christ and declare that He was only a man, a great and good man, yet only a man.

The Scriptures ascribe divine *names* to Christ. "In

the beginning was the Word, and the Word was with God, *and the Word was God*" (John 1:1). (*Word* means Jesus Christ.) "Christ came, who is over all, God blessed forever" (Rom. 9:5). "Unto the Son He saith, Thy throne, *O God*, is for ever and ever" (Heb. 1:8). "Thomas answered and said unto Him, My Lord and my God" (John 20:28). "His Son Jesus Christ. This is the true God, and eternal life" (1 John 5:20). (See also Titus 2:13.)

The Scriptures ascribe divine *attributes* to Him. He is declared to be *eternal* (Col. 1:17; John 1:2; Rev. 1:18); *immutable* (Heb. 1:12; 13:8; 2 Cor. 1:19); *omnipresent* (Matt. 28:20; 18:20; Eph. 1:23); *omniscient* (John 2:25; 1:48; Rev. 2:18); *omnipotent* (Matt. 28:18; Phil. 3:21; Heb. 1:3).

The Scriptures ascribe divine *works* to Him. He forgives sin: See Mark 2:7. He is sent to save sinners: See Matt. 1:21. He shall raise the dead on the last day: See John 6:39. He will judge the world: See John 5:22-23.

The Scriptures ascribe divine *worship* to Him. "All men should honor the Son, even as they honor the Father. He that honoreth not the Son honoreth not the Father which hath sent Him" (John 5:23). "That at the name of Jesus every knee should bow, of things in heaven, and things in earth, and things under the earth; and that every tongue should confess that Jesus is Lord, to the glory of God the Father" (Phil. 2:10-11). (See also Rev. 5:12-14).

Thus we see that Jesus Christ is not only a great and good man He is true God. He is "God manifest in the flesh" (1 Tim. 3:16). To see Him is to see God. "He that hath seen me hath seen the Father" (John 14:9).

He is not the best man, merely; He is the God-man. He was conceived by the Holy Spirit in the womb of a virgin. "The Holy Spirit shall come upon thee, and the power of the Highest shall overshadow thee: therefore also that holy thing which shall be born of thee shall be called the *Son of God*" (Luke 1:35). He has a human nature because His mother was human; He has a divine nature because He is begotten of the Father from eternity. There is mystery here which reason cannot fathom. But while reason cannot grasp it, faith can accept it.

Jesus Christ claimed that He was true God and one with the Father. He called Himself "The only-begotten Son of God" (Son in a sense in which no one else is the son of God). He accepted without protest the adoration of Thomas, who fell before Him, saying, "My Lord and my God." "Jesus said unto them, Verily, verily, I say unto you, Before Abraham was, I am" (John 8:58). He claimed to have the prerogative of forgiving sin. When accused before Pilate of having made such divine claims, He admitted the truth of the charge.

When the Jews once (see John 10:31) took up stones to stone Him "because that Thou being a man, makest Thyself God," He did not deny that He had made this claim, but represented further proof of His divine claim. Jesus Christ made a claim that He was true God. If, as some say, He was not true God, then one of two things must be the case; *either* He was a dreamer, a kindly, self-deceived fool, *or* He was the most colossal deceiver, pretender, and blasphemer that the world has ever known. No other alternative remains. To say that He was a good man, the best man that ever lived, and deny His deity, is absurd.

Either He was what He claimed to be, or the Pharisees were right. He blasphemed God, and then, according to the Mosaic law, He deserved to die.

But we know that He was neither a dreamer nor a deceiver. He was the Son of God, begotten of the Father from eternity. We say with Peter, "Thou art the Christ, the Son of the living God." We bow down with Thomas and say, "My Lord and my God."

The miracles which Christ performed are also a proof of His deity. Winds and waves and all the forces of nature, and even devils, obeyed His word of command. He showed that He was Lord of life and death. He healed the sick, opened the eyes of the blind and the ears of the deaf, cleansed the lepers, and raised the dead. These miracles He was able to do by His own power, and not in the name of another, as His disciples did. The greatest miracle was the resurrection. He was "declared to be the Son of God with power, according to the spirit of holiness, by the resurrection from the dead" (Rom. 1:4).

Christ had this divine power at all times while He was here on earth but He did not always use this power. "He humbled Himself, and became obedient unto death, even the death of the cross" (Phil. 2:8). He laid aside His divine power while He was here, except, for instance, when He performed miracles to prove His divine claims and to help those in distress. This temporary laying aside of His omnipotent power in the state of humiliation explains such Scripture passages as "The Father is greater than I" (John 14:28).

THE SINLESS SAVIOR

Although Jesus Christ was true man, He was *without sin*. He "was in all points tempted like as we are, yet without sin" (Heb. 4:15). Peter, who was with the Lord constantly for three years, declares, "Who did no sin, neither was guile found in His mouth" (1 Peter 2:22). Pilate, after examining the charges brought against Him, gives the verdict, "I find no fault in Him." Judas, in his despair, cries, "I have betrayed innocent blood." Christ is indeed "The Lamb without blemish and without spot." He never in anything that He said or did fell below what one would expect to find in God Himself. The disciples who were with Him daily came at last to understand and believe that this was the Son of God. No mere man could have lived such a sinless life; no mere man could have performed His miracles. He was such a man that we cannot put Him in the same classification with other men. He was the Son of God and the Son of Mary, the God-Man.

THE MERCIFUL SAVIOR

But Jesus was not only mighty, majestic, and pure. He was a kind, loving, tender-hearted and self-sacrificing Savior. He was always moved with pity for men's bodily need as well as for their spiritual distress. Early and late "He went about doing good." His very name means *Savior*. "Thou shalt call His name Jesus: for He shall save His people from their sins" (Matt. 1:21). In order to save us He was willing to suffer as no man ever suffered. "He is despised and rejected of men; a man of sorrows, and acquainted with grief" (Is. 53:3). He endured the ingratitude of the Jews, the false accusations of their religious leaders, the treachery of His own inner circle, the denial of Peter, and the cowardice of the other disciples. "He came unto His own, and His own received Him not" (John 1:11). More pain and disappointment and heartache was crowded into His short life than into a thousand life times. On Good Friday they cry, "Away with Him, Crucify, Crucify." All about Him was like a surging sea of hatred, but His only answer was, "Father, forgive them, for they know not what they do." Through it all, Christ had one great purpose: to save sinners. Christ is holy and mighty. But above all, He is love. He is the Redeemer for whom our hearts yearn.

> Beautiful Savior, King of Creation,
> Son of God and Son of man;
> Truly I'd love Thee, truly I'd serve Thee,
> Light of my soul, my joy, my crown.

> Beautiful Savior, Lord of the nations,
> Son of God and Son of man;
> Glory and honor, praise, adoration,
> Now and forevermore be Thine.

QUESTIONS

What did God do in order that He might save the lost world? What moved God to do this? When was the first promise of the Savior given? How many does God's offer of salvation include? How do we know that Jesus Christ, the Savior, is true man? How do we know that He is true God? What is the significance for us of the sinlessness of the Savior? What is the meaning of the name Jesus?

CHAPTER FIVE

THE SAVIOR'S WORK

Jesus Christ saved us by His perfect obedience to the law of God and by His suffering and death, whereby He atoned for our sins. This was His work. The law had to be kept and the punishment for sin had to be suffered if God should be just and yet justify the sinner. To do this in our stead and on our behalf was the work of our Savior.

HIS PERFECT OBEDIENCE

Christ fulfilled the law for us. The justice of God required that His law be obeyed. In the perfect obedience of Christ the law was kept by man for man. Thus we see that Christ was saving us every day as He overcame all temptations. By His perfect obedience, as well as by His suffering, the requirement of God's justice is vindicated.

It is evident that a sinner could not save the world. The "Lamb" to be slain for our sins must be "without blemish and without spot" (1 Peter 1:19). Because He was conceived by the Holy Spirit, and because He kept the law perfectly, He is indeed "the spotless Lamb of God."

We need a perfect righteousness when we stand in the presence of God. Only Jesus possesses this righteousness, because only He has kept the law perfectly. But He obeyed as our substitute. His obedience was vicarious obedience just as we shall find that His suffering was vicarious suffering. But we who have no righteousness of our own can avail ourselves of

Christ's righteousness. This is the "wedding garment" that has been provided for us (Matt. 22:11). "For as by one man's disobedience [Adam's] many were made sinners, so by the obedience of one [Christ] shall many be made righteous" (Rom. 5:19). (See also Rom. 3:22 and 1 Cor. 1:30).

HIS SUFFERING AND DEATH

We know of the terrible suffering of Jesus Christ. We know that He was bound, smitten, scourged, and nailed to the cross. Besides the pain in body, He suffered unspeakable anguish of soul in Gethsemane when "His sweat was as great drops of blood," and on the cross when He cried, "My God, my God, why hast Thou forsaken me?" What was the purpose and meaning of this suffering? Wherein lies the saving power of the cross? How does the cross save? We must let God give the answer in His Word, the Bible.

We shall give here a number of passages from the Bible which explain the meaning of the cross:

Isa. 53:4, 5, 6, 8, 12, "Surely He [the Messiah] hath borne our griefs, and carried our sorrows ... He was wounded for our transgressions, He was bruised for our iniquities; the chastisement of our peace was upon Him; and with His stripes we are healed ... the Lord hath laid on Him the iniquity of us all ... for the transgression of my people was He stricken ... He bare the sin of many."

Matt. 20:28. "The Son of man came ... to give His life a ransom for many."

John 1:29. "Behold the Lamb of God, which taketh away the sin of the world."

Rom. 5:10. "When we were enemies, we were reconciled to God by the death of His Son."

2 Cor. 5:14. "If one died for all, then were all dead."

2 Cor. 5:21. "Him who knew no sin He made to be sin on our behalf; that we might become the righteousness of God in Him."

2 Cor. 5:18. "God, who hath reconciled us to Himself by Jesus Christ."

Heb. 2:9. "That He ... should taste death for every man."

Rom. 3:25. "Whom God hath set forth to be a propitiation through faith in His blood."

1 Tim. 2:6. "Who gave Himself a ransom for all."

Heb. 9:14. "Who ... offered Himself without spot to God."

1 Peter 2:24. "Who His own self bare our sins in His own body on the tree [the cross] ... by whose stripes ye were healed."

1 Peter 3:18. "Christ also hath once suffered for sins, the just for the unjust, that He might bring us to God, being put to death in the flesh, but quickened by the Spirit."

Heb. 7:27. "Who needeth not daily ... offer up sacrifice ... for this He did once, when He offered up Himself."

1 John 2:2. "He is the propitiation for our sins: and not for ours only, but also for the sins of the whole world."

1 John 4:10. "He loved us, and sent His Son to be the propitiation for our sins."

Rom. 5:9. "Much more then, being now justified by His blood, we shall be saved from wrath through Him."

Eph. 1:7. "In whom we have redemption through His blood, the forgiveness of sins, according to the riches of His grace."

Col. 1:14. "In whom we have redemption through His blood, even the forgiveness of sins."

1 John 1:7. "The blood of Jesus Christ His Son cleanseth us from all sin."

We observe four things as we study these passages of Scripture:

First, that Christ suffered as our *substitute.* His suffering was *vicarious,* that is, it was in our stead, as well as on our behalf. "If one died for all, then were all dead" (2 Cor. 5:14).

Second, that by His suffering Christ atoned for all our sins. (See Heb. 7:27 quoted above.) He is a "propitiation" for the sins of the world, and He gave His life a "ransom" for all. "We were reconciled to God by the death of His Son" (Rom. 5:10). "The Lord hath laid on Him the iniquity of us all" (Isa. 53:6). And the sacrifice made by Christ outweighs, in the sight of God, the sins of the world.

Third, by His suffering Christ atoned for *all sinners as well as for all sins.* He is a propitiation for the sins "of the whole world." He gave Himself "a ransom for all" and His blood "cleanseth from all sin."

Fourth, the perfect sacrifice which Christ made, "His holy and precious blood and His innocent sufferings and death," is the only ground of peace with God and the sinner's only hope. "Much more then, being now justified by *His blood,* we shall be saved from wrath through him" (Rom.5:9). See also Eph. 1:7, quoted above.

> Just as I am, without one plea,
> But that Thy blood was shed for me.

The atonement for the sins of the world made by the vicarious suffering and death of Jesus Christ is the most essential doctrine in God's great plan for saving men. This must ever be kept in the foreground. Our eyes must be fixed on the cross. In our personal faith as well as in our teaching and preaching "we must never wander far from the fountain of blood." In the degree that the cross is in the background in one's faith, in that degree his faith is false; if it is not in his faith at all, his faith is vain. Christianity with the great fact of atonement left out is a shadow or an empty shell. The atonement is the heart of the gospel, and the keystone of the religion of Christ.

We state this with such emphasis because so many deny or at least pass by this most important article of faith. Certain denominations have never included this doctrine in their creeds; such as the Unitarian, Universalist and Christian Science churches. But even in other denominations not a few have come to reject or neglect this fundamental truth. They make of Christ only another martyr, who suffered death for His convictions. We are saved when we try to follow His example. They teach salvation by character instead of by faith in the blood shed on the cross for our sins. Thus they "wring the blood of the gospel" and despise this "blood theology," as they in derision call the atonement. As in the days of the apostle Paul, the preaching of "Christ crucified" is "to the Jews a stumbling block and unto the Greeks, foolishness" (1 Cor. 1:23).

Nevertheless we know that the Scriptures plainly teach that "He was wounded for our transgressions, He was bruised for our iniquities: the chastisement of our peace was upon Him; and with His stripes we are healed." "While we were yet enemies we were reconciled to God by the death of His Son." And when men learn to know their true condition, their great guilt, then they are hungry for this message. It is the gospel that this guilt-laden world needs. The anxious soul finds peace in the knowledge that full atonement has been made for all his sin and that the requirements of God's justice have all been satisfied. This is the rock foundation upon which we build our hope of life eternal. The preaching of "Christ crucified" is foolishness and a stumbling block to our modern Jews and Greeks, but as in the days of old, "to them which are called, both Jews and Greeks, it is the power of God and the wisdom of God." When sinners can lay hold on this comfort, that God will forgive their sins because Christ has made full atonement for all sin on the cross, the deepest need of their being is satisfied and the burden of their sin rolls away. To such the cross becomes great and glorious. With thankful hearts they sing:

> In the cross of Christ I glory,
> Towering o'er the wrecks of time;
> All the light of sacred story
> Gathers round its head sublime.

———————

QUESTIONS

What is meant by Christ's vicarious obedience? What is meant by Christ's vicarious suffering and death? What place must the cross of Christ have in our faith? How does Christ's suffering differ from martyrdom? What comfort does the death of Christ bring to a troubled soul?

CHAPTER SIX

THE HOLY SPIRIT

THE PERSON OF THE HOLY SPIRIT

As already stated in Chapter Two, the Bible ascribes divine names, divine attributes, divine works, and divine worship to the Holy Spirit (also called Holy Ghost). The Holy Spirit is plainly called God in Acts 5:3-4. "Why hath Satan filled thine heart to lie to the Holy Spirit? ... thou hast not lied unto men, but unto God." The Spirit is called Jehovah in 2 Sam. 23:2. He is called Lord in 2 Cor. 3:17. He is declared to be eternal in Heb. 9:14, "Christ, who through the eternal Spirit offered Himself without blemish unto God." He is declared to be omniscient in 1 Cor. 2:10, "The Spirit searcheth all things, yea, the deep things of God." A divine work is also ascribed to the Spirit in the miraculous conception of Jesus (Luke 1:35).

The Bible teaches that the Holy Spirit is a person distinct from the Father and the Son, and not only the power or the will or the intelligence of the Father, as some claim. He is not only a different form or mode in which God manifests Himself. The distinction between the Holy Spirit and the Father and the Son is real and personal, not only a difference in manifestation. When the Bible speaks of the Holy Spirit, this is not only a personification of the power of God. Personal works are ascribed to the Holy Spirit. He teaches: John 14:26. He speaks: Acts 1:16. He comforts: Acts 9:31. He strives with sinners: Gen. 6:3. He testifies of Christ: John 15:26. He sanctifies: Rom. 15:16. He can be grieved: Eph. 4:30. Note also that the Bible calls the

Holy Spirit "He," not "it" (See John 16:8; 16:14). And at the baptism of Jesus there was a revelation of the Holy Spirit separate and distinct from the revelation of the Father and the Son (Matt. 3:16).

But while the Holy Spirit is a distinct person in the Trinity, He is coordinated with the Father and the Son. The three persons are equal, and not one above or below the others. In Matt. 28:19 we see that baptism is to be administered in His name as well as in the name of the Father and of the Son. Likewise in the Apostolic Benediction the Holy Spirit is coordinated with the other two persons in the Godhead. "The grace of the Lord Jesus Christ, and the love of God, and the communion of the Holy Spirit, be with you all" (2 Cor. 13:14). The presence of the Holy Spirit together with the Father and the Son at the baptism of Jesus also indicates that the three persons are equal.

THE WORK OF THE HOLY SPIRIT

By His holy life and His atoning death, Christ has provided salvation for all men. But by nature man is "dead in trespasses and sins" (Eph. 2:1). Man must be made willing and able to avail himself of the salvation so graciously provided in Christ. It is the task of the Holy Spirit to work repentance and faith in the hearts of men so that they will "believe in Jesus Christ and come to Him." Thus the Holy Spirit applies redemption to men's souls. And this work which the Holy Spirit does within our hearts is as important as the work which Christ did for us when He died for us on the cross.

The work of the Holy Spirit is more fully stated in the Third Article of the Apostles' Creed.

THE THIRD ARTICLE

OF SANCTIFICATION

I believe in the Holy Ghost; the holy Christian Church, the communion of saints; the forgiveness of sins; the resurrection of the body, and the life everlasting. Amen.

What is meant by this?

I believe that I cannot by my own reason or strength believe in Jesus Christ my Lord, or come to Him; but the Holy Ghost has called me by the gospel, enlightened me with His gifts, and sanctified and preserved me in the true faith; even as He calls, gathers, enlightens and sanctifies the whole Christian church on earth, and preserves it in union with Jesus Christ in the one true faith; in which Christian church He daily and richly forgives me and all believers all our sins, and at the last day will raise up me and all the dead, and will grant me and all believers in Christ everlasting life. This is most certainly true.

REPENTANCE

In the sense in which we use repentance here it means sorrow for sin or contrition. "It is with heartfelt contrition and sorrow to acknowledge our sins and honestly to confess them before God" (S.208). Compare the penitence of David, as expressed in Psalm 51; of Peter, in Luke 22:62; of the publican, in Luke 18:13. Not everyone will have the overwhelming sense of guilt and the same degree of contrition as the three examples just cited. But always there must be a sense of need and helplessness, and the willingness to say, "Nothing in my hands I bring." We must acknowledge that we have deserved God's wrath and condemnation. We must humble ourselves before Him and be willing to confess and forsake sin. For "they that be whole need not a physician; but they that are sick" (Luke 5:31). Only such a penitent soul will care for salvation and long for a share in redemption.

This power to repent comes from the Holy Spirit. He calls and enlightens us by the Word of God. He impresses upon us the requirements of God's holy law. Thus the law becomes "our schoolmaster to bring us unto Christ" (Gal. 3:24). By our own reason or strength we are utterly unable to come to Christ or to believe. But the Holy Spirit makes men see and acknowledge their guilt and long for the mercy of God. "The sacrifices of God are a broken spirit: a broken and contrite heart, O God, Thou wilt not despise" (Psalm 51:17).

FAITH

The Holy Spirit comforts the penitent sinner with the glad tidings of God's grace in Jesus Christ, and enables him to "believe in Jesus Christ and come to Him." He gives the contrite sinner power to accept Christ in a true and living faith. Saving faith consists in this, "that a penitent soul lays hold on Jesus Christ as his only Savior from sin, death, and the power of the devil; and that he seeks his only refuge in Him and His merits, and with intimate confidence relies on Him" (S. 212). The faith that saves does not consist merely in holding certain doctrines concerning Christ to be true, although having the true doctrines is important. Only to know the history of Christ as told in the Bible and to believe this to be a true story, is not saving faith. But when an anxious soul believes that Christ has come to save him, and he stakes everything on Him, trusting Him to carry him through in life and death, it is faith. Faith thus is a personal acceptance of Jesus Christ as one's Savior, and the surrender of one's life to Him. This trust in Christ as Savior is worked in our hearts by the power of the Holy Spirit. "No man can say that Jesus is the Lord, but by the Holy Spirit" (1 Cor. 12:3). When the Spirit has brought us to this attitude of surrender to Christ and trust in Him, then we no longer know these things about the Savior as a matter of information alone, but as a matter of personal experience. Examples: Luke 19:1-10; Acts 16: 25-35; Luke 7:37-50.

The nature of faith, as we have just seen, is trust, childlike trust. The *object* of our faith, that in which we trust, is Jesus Christ — Christ Himself, His righteousness and His atonement for our sin. Faith itself has no merit; it earns nothing and deserves nothing. The value of faith comes from that on which it lays hold, namely, Christ and His merit. Faith is only the hand held out to receive the gift of God's grace in Christ.

The experiences of repentance and faith described here together constitute conversion.

True faith is not equally strong in all persons, nor equally strong at all times. There are times when the sinner hardly dares to appropriate God's grace. But even a weak faith has full salvation, as long as it is characterized by an earnest hatred of sin and a deep longing for grace. For it is not because of our faith that we really are saved, but because of the righteousness and atonement of Jesus Christ on which faith lays hold. And Christ's work is the same whether the hand of faith by which we accept this gift is weak or strong. God says, "A bruised reed shall He not break, and the smoking flax shall He not quench" (Isa. 42:3). God also accepts those who can only say, "I believe, Lord, help Thou my unbelief" (Mark 9:24). However, we should not be content with a weak faith. It may so easily be lost. And we do not experience the joy of the Christian life unless we have the assurance of salvation. Therefore we should pray God to strengthen our faith.

By the faith which the Holy Spirit works in the heart the believer is justified and born again.

JUSTIFICATION

Justification is "an act of God by which He accounts or judges a sinner righteous in His sight." It means a change in God's way of looking at the sinner, a new judgment passed upon him. Every debt of sin is wiped out. "God by grace imputes Christ's righteousness to a penitent and believing sinner; acquits him of sin and its punishment; and regards him in Christ as if he had never sinned" (S. 218). "Him who knew no sin He made to be sin on our behalf; that we might become the righteousness of God in Him" (2 Cor. 5:21).

JUSTIFICATION THROUGH GRACE, NOT MERIT

The Word of God says, "By *grace* are ye saved through faith; and that not of yourselves: it is the gift of God: not of works, lest any man should boast" (Eph. 2:8-9). The Scriptures also declare: "That no man is justified by the law in the sight of God is evident; for the just shall live by faith" (Gal. 3:11). "To him that worketh not, but believeth on Him that justifieth the ungodly. his faith is counted for righteousness" (Rom. 4:5). From these verses, and a great many others like them, it is very evident the sinner never merits salvation. He can never, by his own works, become just toward God. "For this purpose our best works are of no use at all; we build the hope of our salvation alone upon Christ and His merits" (S. 232). That which moves God to save us is solely His grace. The way of salvation is not, "Be good and you will be saved," "Do the best you can and you will be saved." This would be building on our works, but the way is, "Believe on the Lord Jesus Christ, and thou shalt be saved" (Acts 16:31). There is no justification by works. Justification is by faith through grace. The sinner must learn to say:

> Nothing in my hands I bring,
> Simply to Thy cross I cling.

We can make no plea on the basis of any merit which we possess. We can only say:

> Just as I am, without one plea,
> But that Thy blood was shed for me,
> And that Thou bidst me come to Thee,
> O Lamb of God, I come, I come.

Besides the passages quoted in the above paragraph, see also all of the Epistle to the Galatians; Romans, chapters three to eight; John 3:16; Eph. 2:8; and a great many other passages.

REGENERATION, OR THE NEW BIRTH

By nature man is "dead in trespasses and sins" (Eph. 2:1; Col. 2:13). As we are born into this world we do not have "life everlasting." Jesus says, "Whatsoever is born of the flesh, is flesh" (John 3:6). As there has been a birth of the flesh so there must also be a birth "of the Spirit." "Whatsoever is born of the Spirit, is spirit" (John 3:6). Jesus says, "Ye must be born again" (John 3:7). "Verily, verily, I say unto you, except a man be born of the water and the Spirit, he cannot enter the kingdom of God" (John 3:5). It is not merely improvement in our conduct that we need. We need a new life within. A man may be respectable and upright in his conduct and still not have this new life. Nicodemus was an upright man. But Christ told him that what he needed was a new life within, the life that is "born of the Spirit" (John 3:1-9; 2 Cor. 5:17; Col. 3:10; 1 Peter 1:23; 1 John 5:18; Ezek. 11:19).

The new birth (regeneration) is an act of the Holy Spirit by which new spiritual life is imparted to man. This new life is "everlasting life." It cannot be harmed by disease, old age, or anything that is physical or material. No mental or moral effort on the part of man can endow him with this new life. Nor is it attained by any evolution of character. It is bestowed upon us by an act of the Holy Spirit as He works through Word and sacrament. (See discussion of the means of grace in Chapter Eight of this Manual).

THE HOLY SPIRIT CAN BE RESISTED

As the Holy Spirit calls men, He also offers them power to obey the call. He not only seeks to persuade men to come to Christ and believe in Him, but through the means of grace He also bestows the power to believe. But so many resist the Holy Spirit and will not repent and come to Christ. "Ye do always resist the Holy Spirit" (Acts 7:51). "I have spread out my hands all the day unto a rebellious people" (Isa. 65:2). "O Jerusalem, Jerusalem, thou that killest the prophets, and stonest them which are sent unto thee, how often would I have gathered thy children together, even as a hen gathereth her chickens under her wings, *and ye would not!*" (Matt. 23:37). Man cannot help God in any way, *but he can hinder Him.* We give God all the glory when a sinner is saved. But man must bear the whole blame and responsibility if he is lost. "The Lord is merciful and gracious, slow to anger, and plenteous in mercy" (Ps. 103:8). But if men resist the Holy Spirit, and will not repent and believe, they are forever lost. "How shall we escape, if we neglect so great salvation?" (Heb. 2:3). "Today if ye will hear His voice, harden not your hearts " (Heb. 4:7).

QUESTIONS

How do we know that the Holy Spirit is a person distinct from the Father and the Son? What is the special work of the Holy Spirit? What is repentance? What is faith in Christ? Whence comes the power to repent? Whence comes the power to believe in Christ? On what does faith lay hold? What is the nature or essence of faith? What is conversion? How can weak faith be saving faith? What is justification? What is the meaning of grace? What is regeneration? Can the Holy Spirit be resisted?

CHAPTER SEVEN

HOW THE HOLY SPIRIT SANCTIFIES THE BELIEVER

The Holy Spirit sanctifies the believer in Christ. "Sanctification (in the narrow sense) is that gracious act of the Holy Spirit by which He daily more and more renews the believer after the image of God" (S. 229).

THE IMPORTANCE OF HOLINESS

The grace of God must not be made an excuse for sin. "What shall we say then? Shall we continue in sin, that grace may abound? God forbid. Shall we, that are dead to sin, live any longer therein?" (Rom. 6:1-2.) "Be ye therefore perfect, even as your Father which is in heaven is perfect" (Matt. 5:48). This is the goal toward which all Christians must strive. Faith that does not result in a holy life and deeds of love is only a dead faith. "As the body without the spirit is dead, so faith without works is dead" (James 2:26). "Do we then make void the law through faith? God forbid" (Rom. 3:31). "Let your light so shine before men, that they may see your good works, and glorify your Father which is in heaven" (Matt. 5:16). "If ye love me, keep my commandments" (John 14:15). "The fruit of the Spirit is love, joy, peace, longsuffering, gentleness, goodness, faith, meekness, temperance: against such there is no law" (Gal. 5:22-23). Christians must grow in grace. Being in grace, they must grow therein (Eph. 4:20-24; 2 Peter 3:18).

The Christian experiences that there is a conflict within him between the new life (called the new man) and the old, sinful nature (called the old man). "The flesh lusts against the Spirit and the Spirit against the flesh" (Gal. 5:17). More or less, this is the experience of all. "The good that I would, this I do not, but the evil which I would not, that I do" (Rom. 7:19). "I delight in the law of God after the inward man: but I see another law in my members" (Rom. 7:22-23). "God's children hate evil, and heartily seek to obey His commands; but it is their daily experience that they sin, and that their new life is weak" (S.107). Christians seek to obey Christ's words when He said, "If any man will come after me, let him deny himself, take up his cross, and follow me" (Matt. 16:24). Christians endeavor in all things to do the will of God. They fight constantly against the devil, the world, and the flesh. They are deeply grieved when they find that they have sinned. They ask God's forgiveness and earnestly seek to put away their sins (S. 108).

God shows believers how they should live in His holy law, the Ten Commandments (See Chapter Three).

The summary of all the commandments is love; love to God, love to ourselves, and love to our neighbor (S.17). "Love is the fulfilling of the law" (Rom. 13:10). "Thou shalt love the Lord thy God with all thy heart, and with all thy soul, and with all thy strength, and with all thy mind" (Luke 10:27). "Thou shalt love thy neighbor as thyself" (Matt. 22:39). See also Matt. 5:44-46 and Matt. 7:12 (the Golden Rule). "The end of the commandment is love" (1 Tim. 1:5).

CHRIST, THE PATTERN

We must seek to obey the law as Christ interpreted it and as He Himself kept it. Christ is the pattern and example for Christians. We are to be *Christlike*. Christ shows us what we ought to be and do. We are "to walk even as He walked" (1 John 2:6). He left us "an example. that ye should follow His steps" (1 Peter 2:21). Like our Lord, we are not only to be good, but we are to do good. Of Him it is said, "He went about doing good" (Acts 10:38). So also must we. We are not to be "Do-nothing saints." We are to serve Christ in serving our fellowmen when they in any way need our help (Matt. 25:35-36).

Christ also strongly emphasized that the law must be kept in the heart. It is not to the hand God says, "Thou shalt not steal or kill." But to the heart. "Whosoever looketh on a woman to lust after her hath committed adultery with her already in his heart" (Matt.5:28). It is the same with all the commandments; they must be kept in the heart. "Keep thy heart with all diligence; for out of it are the issues of life" (Prov. 4:23).

We know that we are not saved by the law (Compare Chapter Six). The law is a mirror revealing our sins, and thus it alarms us and drives us to Christ (Rom. 3:19, Gal. 3:24). But more than this, the law shows believers the fruits that faith should bear (S. 16). "Thy law is a lamp unto my feet, and a light unto my path" (Ps. 119:105).

THE MOTIVE

We should keep the law, not in order to become Christians, *but because we are Christians*. Not the fear of punishment, but the love of God should be the motive of obedience. "The love of Christ constraineth us" (2 Cor.5:14). "If ye love me, keep my commandments" (John 14:15). Love to God and the desire to glorify Him should move us to obey. "Let your light so shine before men, that they may see your good works, and *glorify your Father* which is in heaven" (Matt. 5:16).

While we should strive for perfect holiness and never be satisfied with imperfection, still we know that our sanctification never becomes perfect here below. "If we say that we have no sin, we deceive ourselves, and the truth is not in us" (1 John 1:8). As long as we live we will need to pray the prayer which Christ gave us for our constant use, "Forgive us our trespasses as we forgive those who trespass against us." "Not as though I had already attained, either were already perfect: but I follow after, if that I may apprehend that for which also I am apprehended of Christ Jesus" (Phil. 3:12).

In order to grow in the grace of sanctification, we must always seek to obey the promptings of the Holy Spirit within us. We must diligently use the means of grace, Word and sacraments. We must watch and pray, and thus constantly seek and rely on the help of God.

PRAYER

Prayer is as necessary for spiritual life as breathing is for the life of the body. He who does not pray is not a Christian. "God fades out of the life of the man who does not pray." We should look upon it as a privilege to ask God for His mercy and help, and a pleasure to thank Him, not merely as a duty. We should pray in the morning, each day speaking to God before we speak to men. At the close of each day we should return thanks to God for His many kindnesses and ask for pardon for our sins. And often during the day we should lift up our hearts to God in prayer and praise.

But our prayers must not be mere words, or parrot-like repetitions of pious phrases. The essence of prayer is the deep desire of the heart. Words which do not express the longing of the heart for God and His help are not prayer.

> Prayer is the soul's sincere desire,
> Unuttered or expressed;
> The motion of a hidden fire
> That trembles in the breast.
>
> Prayer is the burden of a sigh,
> The falling of a tear,
> The upward glancing of the eye
> When none but God is near.

The model prayer is the Lord's Prayer. The disciples of Jesus came to Him and said, "Lord, teach us to pray, as John also taught his disciples. And He answered and said unto them, When ye pray, say, Our Father who art in heaven, etc." Then He gave them this prayer:

Our Father, who art in heaven; Hallowed be Thy name; Thy kingdom come; Thy will be done on earth, as it is in heaven; Give us this day our daily bread; and forgive us our trespasses as we forgive those who trespass against us; and lead us not into temptation; but deliver us from evil; for Thine is the kingdom, and the power, and the glory, for ever and ever. Amen.

We should pray to the triune God alone and in the name of Jesus. "And whatsoever ye shall ask in my name, that will I do, that the Father may be glorified in the Son" (John 14:15). To pray in His name means that we realize our own unworthiness to receive that for which we ask and base our plea for help on Jesus' merits alone. And we should ask in faith, "Let him ask in faith, nothing wavering. For he that wavereth is like a wave of the sea driven with the wind and tossed. For let not that man think that he shall receive anything of the Lord" (James 1:6-7).

The prayer of faith made in the name of Christ has promise of answer. If we do not ask for that which would be harmful, God will surely answer, in His own time and way. "Ask and it shall be given you, seek and ye shall find; knock and it shall be opened unto you" (Matt. 7:7). See James 5:16; Eph.. 3:20; John 14:14; Ps. 91:15; 50:15; Matt. 21:22; Luke 18:7; 1 John 3:22.

QUESTIONS

Mention some of the fruits which faith will bear. What is meant by "the old man"? What is meant by "new man"? What is the summary of all the commandments? What is the true pattern for the Christian's conduct? What is the true motive for Christ-like conduct? What means will help us to lead a godly life? What is it to pray? What does it mean to pray in the name of Jesus?

CHAPTER EIGHT

THE MEANS OF GRACE

GOD'S USE OF MEANS

God purposed to save sinful mankind. So He sent His Son Jesus Christ to be the Savior of the world. Through Him and His work forgiveness of sin, life and salvation were provided. God desires to bestow this salvation upon us.

But God bestows His grace through certain *means*. These are called the *means of grace*. There are three means of grace: the Word of God, Baptism, and the Lord's Supper. It is through these means (vehicles or vessels) that God's grace ordinarily is brought to man. Through these means God imparts life, and nourishes, strengthens and preserves life.

No one denies that God could give us His grace without means, by a mere act of His will. In like manner He could impart and maintain the life of the body without means. But it has pleased Him to use means in both instances. God ordinarily carries out His purposes through means and He has bound us to the use of these means.

That God works through these means appears from the condition of the heathen. Before missionaries go out to the heathen with the means of grace, the Word and the sacraments, they remain unchanged in the darkness of sin. But when the missionaries bring the heathen the means of grace, then changes are wrought and sinners are saved. No converted heathen has ever been found where the means of grace had not come. And no other means will do. The Word and the sacraments are the divinely appointed means to bring grace and salvation to the hearts of men. Through these God saves.

THE WORD AS A MEANS OF GRACE

The Word of God as found in the Bible is not only a book of history and instructions. The Word does more than merely give us certain directions regarding what we should believe and do. The Word is a *means of grace*, that is, it brings to us and bestows upon us the grace of God concerning which it teaches. The Holy Spirit is present in and with the Word, giving it divine power and making it a vessel or channel that brings the grace of God (faith, forgiveness of sins, eternal life, and spiritual power) to man. The Word both imparts life and nourishes the new life. "Being born again, not of corruptible seed, but of incorruptible, *by the Word of God*, which liveth and abideth forever" (1 Peter 1:23). "The words that I speak unto you, they are spirit, and they are life" (John 6:63). "Man shall not live by bread alone, but by every word that proceedeth out of the mouth of God" (Matt. 4:4). See also Heb. 4:12, "For the Word of God is quick, and powerful, etc.," and Eph.. 6:17, "The sword of the Spirit, which is the Word of God."

There is always power (efficacy) in the Word of God. Man may neglect or resist the Word and reject the salvation it offers and bestows. But this does not prove that there is no power in the Word any more than refusing to take food would show that there is no nourishment in it. The Word is at all times a means of grace, but one can resist its power and lose its blessing.

The Sacraments as Means of Grace

The Word of God may come to us without any rite or ceremony, or it may be accompanied by a divinely ordained rite, as in the sacraments. "A sacrament is a holy act instituted by God, in which by visible means, He bestows and seals His invisible grace" (S. 333).

Christ has instituted two sacraments, Baptism and Holy Communion, or the Lord's Supper. There are two factors in each sacrament, the divine and invisible gift, and the earthly, visible sign.

These sacraments are not mere ceremonies, rites, or symbols. They are means of grace. They not merely signify something, but they actually convey that which they signify. They are divinely appointed vessels which convey God's blessed spiritual gifts to us. They are a special way by which God brings us the blessings of His Word. They are an essential part of the plan of salvation.

Christ Himself has instituted the sacraments. (See Matt. 28:19; Luke 22:14 ff., and other passages.) To neglect the sacraments is to despise the plain teaching of Christ and the teaching and example of His apostles. To say that these sacraments are only "foolishness" is to charge Jesus Christ with folly, for He gave them to us. To belittle the sacraments is to belittle an institution of the Son of God.

The sacraments are tokens of God's eternal love. They represent all that Christ has done for us and convey to the individual the salvation of Christ. They individualize the general word of the gospel. In the sacraments the general promise of the gospel concerning forgiveness of sins for Christ's sake is applied and sealed to the individual. They are pledges of God's mercy, that make it easier for the individual to believe the promise of the gospel. "These sacraments bring us the Word of God, and with it the joy, peace, and pardon it confers. They are a promise sealed with solemn, sacred acts which Christ Himself commanded. They give us an assurance on which our faith can rest, and through which our confidence in the heavenly Father's love and mercy can daily grow more strong" (Jacobs: *The Way*, p. 128).

BAPTISM

Baptism was instituted by Jesus Christ. "All authority hath been given unto me in heaven and on earth. Go ye therefore, and make disciples of all the nations, baptizing them into the name of the Father and of the Son and of the Holy Spirit: teaching them to observe all things whatsoever I commanded you" (Matt. 28:18-19). "He that believeth and is baptized shall be saved; but he that believeth not shall be damned" (Mark 16:16). Baptism is also given a prominent place in the teaching and practice of the apostles of Christ. On the great day of Pentecost in Jerusalem many were convicted of sin as Peter spoke, and they asked, "Men and brethren, what shall we do? And Peter said unto them, Repent, and be baptized every one of you in the name of Jesus Christ for the remission of sins, and ye shall receive the gift of the Holy Spirit" (Acts 2:37-38). Acts 8:12 relates that when Philip had preached many believed and "They were baptized, both men and women." Peter preached the gospel in the home of Cornelius. The Holy Spirit came upon those who were gathered there, "And he [Peter] commanded them to be baptized in the name of the Lord" (Acts 10:48). The Philippian jailer fell down before Paul and Silas and asked, "Sirs, what must I do to be saved? And they said, Believe on the Lord Jesus Christ, and thou shalt be saved, and thy house ... And he took them the same hour of the night, and washed their stripes; and was baptized, he and all his, straightway" (Acts 16:30-31, 33). These are only some of the examples that show what a prominent place baptism was given in the teaching and practice of Christ and His apostles.

Some ask, What good can a little water do? "Baptism is not simply water, it is the water comprehended in God's command and connected with God's Word" (Luther's Catechism). It is a use of water which God has commanded and concerning which He has given a promise. "It is not water indeed that does it, but the Word of God which is in and with the water. For without the Word of God the water is simply water and no baptism. But with the Word of God it is a baptism, that is a gracious water of life and a washing of regeneration in the Holy Spirit" (Luther's Catechism). In Titus 3:5 the Word of God says concerning baptism, "According to His mercy He saved us, by the washing of regeneration." It calls it a washing that regenerates, or brings about a new birth. In John 3:5 Christ speaks of being born again "of water and the Spirit." All we who "were baptized into Jesus Christ were baptized into His death" (Rom. 6:3). Through baptism we come to share in the salvation won for us by the death of Christ. "For as many of you as have been baptized into Christ have put on Christ" (Gal. 3:27). Christ and

His righteousness became ours through baptism. Saul at Damascus was told, "Arise, and be baptized, and wash away thy sins" (Acts 22:16). Here, too, we see the great benefit that baptism bestows. (See also 1 Peter 3:21. "Baptism saves us.")

Every person born into the world is by nature a child of wrath (Eph. 2:3). He has no spiritual life. He is flesh born of flesh, nothing more (John 3:6). He is brought forth in iniquity and conceived in sin (Psalm 51:5). He is born with a sinful nature. He needs the gift of eternal life. He needs a Savior. He needs grace. Therefore in obedience to Christ's command we baptize him with water in the name of the triune God. Through this baptism he is united with God, his heavenly Father, and Christ, his Savior, and the Holy Spirit, his Sanctifier. Thus he receives forgiveness of sin, grace, and life eternal. He is no longer a child of wrath, but a child of grace. This is what happens in baptism, nothing less. The child is brought into covenant with God. And the Lord has promised in Isa. 54:10: "The mountains may depart, and the hills be removed; but my lovingkindness shall not depart from thee, neither shall my covenant of peace be removed."

BAPTISM OF CHILDREN

There are those who deny the necessity and validity of infant baptism. While there is no specific command to baptize children, that we should do so follows as a logical conclusion from what is clearly taught in the Scriptures. The main reason for believing in infant baptism is what has already been stated in a previous paragraph of this chapter, namely, the sinful state of every child. Jesus says, "Suffer the little children to come unto me, and forbid them not: for of such is the kingdom of God" (Mark 10:14). By this we see that the little children are to be members of the kingdom of God. But the same Jesus says, "Ye must be born anew." "Except one be born anew, he cannot see the kingdom of God." "That which is born of the flesh is flesh." This does not leave room for any exception. All who are born into the world in the natural course must be born anew before they can enter the kingdom of God. What shall we then do so that a little child, intended for the kingdom of God, may be born anew? Jesus plainly shows us what we are to do when He speaks of being born *of water and the Spirit*" (See John 3:1-8). That this can only mean baptism is also plain from Titus 3:5, which speaks of "the washing of regeneration."

The analogy between baptism and circumcision sustains this teaching and corroborates it. Circumcision was the Old Testament rite of admission into God's covenant. Now, as it was administered to children eight days old, the conclusion is irresistible that baptism ordained by Christ to take the place of circumcision must also be designed for children (Lutheran Manual, p. 47). That circumcision is supplanted by baptism as a mark of the covenant with God is indicated by Col. 2:11-12.

This teaching concerning the necessity and validity of the baptism of children is also corroborated by the instances of the baptism of the whole households which are recorded in the New Testament. (See Acts 16:15, 16:33, 1 Cor. 1:16 and other passages.) There is at least a strong presumption that there were small children in these families.

It is objected that a child cannot have faith and that it is only those who believe and are baptized that are saved. But faith is always the gift of God (Eph. 2:8). It is never a product of our own making. Will anyone say that God can give this faith to an adult, who always offers more or less resistance in whose heart there is much unbelief, but that He cannot give it to a child, who offers no conscious resistance? To say that God cannot give faith to an infant is to limit the power of the Almighty and say, "So far canst Thou go, but no farther." A child does not have a mature or developed faith, but it does receive that which God calls faith. In Mark 10 we are told that Christ took the "little children" in His arms and "blessed" them. The original Greek text plainly shows that these were very young children. But it is plain that they were capable of receiving Christ's blessing. Christ said further that we must all receive the kingdom "as a little child." By this we also see that little children are capable of receiving divine grace.

Note: We do not teach that infants who die unbaptized are condemned. But God has revealed nothing as to the fate of children who die without baptism. He has bound us to the use of the means of grace, but He has not bound Himself. But since nothing has been revealed as to the state of children who die without having been baptized, it is imperative that we bring our little ones early to God in baptism.

THE MODE OF BAPTISM

There has been much discussion as to whether baptism should be by immersion, by sprinkling, or pouring. On this point it is to be noted that the Greek word translated baptize does not necessarily mean to immerse. It can mean that, but it is also used where it cannot possibly mean that (See Mark 7:3; Luke 11:38. Here the same Greek word means wash. Compare 1 Cor. 10:2).

Moreover, no one can prove that a single instance of baptism recorded in the New Testament was by immersion. Usually every circumstance points to sprinkling or pouring. That baptism sometimes might have been by immersion is not denied. That it always was, can never be proved The jailer at Philippi and his family were baptized in the jail at midnight (Acts 16:33). There is not the slightest reference to any larger quantity of water being used. Everything points to sprinkling or pouring. Acts 10:47 tells of the baptism of Cornelius and his household. When Peter saw that the Holy Spirit had been given he said, "Can any man forbid water, that these should not be baptized, who have received the Holy Spirit as well as we?" The words of Peter here certainly indicate the application of the water to the subject, rather than the immersion of the one baptized in the water. Concerning the baptism of Jesus in the Jordan we read, "And Jesus, when He was baptized, went up straightway from the water" (Matt. 3:16). These words certainly indicate nothing as to whether He was immersed in the stream or John poured water on His head. In Acts 8:38-39 we read of the baptism of the eunuch by Philip. "And they went down both into the water, both Philip and the eunuch; and he baptized him. And when *they* [both of them] were come up out of the water, etc." The same is said of both, "they went down into the water — they came up out of the water." There is nothing that proves immersion. In the story of Paul's baptism in Damascus there is not the slightest hint of immersion (Acts 9:18).

Some advocates of immersion have tried to make much of the reference to being "buried with Christ in baptism," found in Rom. 6:4, and Col. 2:12. But when we recall that the body of Christ was not let down into a grave and covered, as we are accustomed to burying, but was placed in a vault in the side of a cliff, then we see at once that the language of these passages proves nothing with reference to immersion.

Sprinkling and pouring were used in the Old Testament as symbols of purification (Numb. 8:5-7. Compare Isa. 52:15; Ezek. 36:25). The New Testament compares baptism to this (John 3:22-26. Compare John 4:1-2. Also compare Joel 2:28 with Acts 1:15. See 1 Cor. 10:2). The natural conclusion from this is that the New Testament writers were familiar with the same form of baptism now used most extensively in the Christian church, namely, sprinkling and pouring.

BAPTISM OF ADULTS

Adults who have not been baptized but who have come to the knowledge of the salvation provided for sinners in Christ, and who want to follow Him, should be baptized. For them not to receive baptism would be to disobey the plain command of Christ. Through their baptism they are brought into covenant with God, and He seals His grace upon them. As circumcision was in the Old Testament, so Baptism in the New Testament is the mark of those who have entered into covenant relation with God.

CONFIRMATION

Confirmation is primarily a confession of faith and a promise to remain true to Christ unto the end. After having been instructed in the Word of God, an opportunity is given in confirmation to confess one's faith. This confession does not only mean that one believes the Word of God and the teaching of a given church; it means also that one has given his heart to Christ and trusts Him for salvation. Thus the covenant with God entered into in baptism is renewed in confirmation. In the solemn service of confirmation the minister lays his hands on each member of the class or group, while the prayers of the assembled congregation go up to God that He will grant steadfastness in the faith even unto death.

It is not claimed that God has specifically commanded this form of confession of faith, nor that this form is essential to salvation. But God has said that where there is faith in the heart, there must also be confession. "If thou shalt confess with thy mouth the Lord Jesus, and shalt believe in thine heart that God hath raised Him from the dead, thou shalt be saved. For with the heart man believeth unto righteousness; and with the mouth confession is made unto salvation" (Rom. 10:9-10). "Whosoever therefore shall confess me before men, him will I confess also before my Father who is in heaven. But whosoever shall deny me before men, him will I also deny before my Father who is in heaven" (Matt. 10:32-33). Thus the Word of God emphasizes the importance of confession. We believe that confirmation is a form of confession which is pleasing to God.

God has commanded the church to teach (Matt. 28:20). In the course of instruction which precedes confirmation we are obeying this divine command. By this instruction in the Word, as well as by confession, faith is strengthened or "confirmed." Confirmation also admits to the Lord's Supper. By the instruction which is given, one is enabled to examine himself as to his worthiness to receive the holy Sacrament (1 Cor. 11:28).

The denominations which have consistently held to the rite of confirmation are the Roman Catholic, the Episcopal and the Lutheran. In these churches confirmation admits to the Lord's Supper and full communicant membership. Various other denominations admit members by a form of confession of faith somewhat like confirmation. However, it differs from the Lutheran practice in one important regard: it is usually not preceded by thorough instruction in the Word of God.

QUESTIONS

Which are the means of grace? Why did Jesus call the Word of God a seed? What is a sacrament? How many sacraments did Christ institute? Which are the two factors in each sacrament? What is the purpose of the sacraments? Quote the words which Christ used when He instituted Baptism. Mention several instances of Baptism in the Apostolic church. What precious gifts are received through Baptism? What is it that gives Baptism its regenerative power? Why do we believe in infant Baptism? Why is immersion not necessary for a valid Baptism? What is the meaning of confirmation?

CHAPTER NINE

THE MEANS OF GRACE

CONTINUED

THE LORD'S SUPPER

The Bible tells of the institution of the Lord's Supper in the following words:

"Our Lord Jesus Christ, in the night in which He was betrayed, took bread, and when He had given thanks, He brake it and gave it to His disciples saying, Take, eat; this is my body which is given for you, this do in remembrance of me."

"After the same manner, also, when He had supped, He took the cup, and when He had given thanks, He gave it to them saying, Drink ye all of it; this cup is the New Testament in my blood, which is shed for you and for many for the remission of sins; this do as oft as ye drink it in remembrance of me" (See Matt. 26:25 ff., Luke 22:14 ff., Mark 14:20 ff., 1 Cor. 11:23 ff).

WHAT THE LORD'S SUPPER IS

"The Lord's Supper (Sacrament of the Altar) is the true body and blood of our Lord Jesus Christ, under bread and wine, instituted by Christ Himself, for us Christians to eat and drink" (Luther's Catechism). It is the Lord's Word which makes the Lord's Supper the sacrament of Christ's body and blood. If the bread and wine were without God's Word, they would be only bread and wine; but being connected with God's Word, they are truly the body and blood of Christ. "For as the mouth of Christ speaketh, so is it. He can neither lie nor deceive."

Our reason cannot tell us what the Lord's Supper is, nor our sense of sight or taste or touch, but only the Word of God. What saith the Scriptures? Concerning the *bread* in this sacrament the Word of God speaks as follows: Matt. 26:26, "Take, eat; this is my body." Mark 14:22, "Take ye: this is my body." Luke 22:19, "This is my body which is given for you." Concerning the *wine* we read: Matt. 26:27-28, "Drink ye all of it; for this is my blood of the covenant, which is poured out for many unto remission of sins." Mark 14:24, "This is my blood of the covenant, which is poured out for many." Luke 22:20, "This cup is the new covenant in my blood, even that which is poured out for you." 1 Cor. 11:25, "This cup is the new covenant in my blood." Four times we read of the bread, "This is my body." Once we read of the wine, "This is my blood." Twice we read, "This is my blood of the covenant." Twice we read, "This cup is the new covenant in my blood." And in 1 Cor. 10:16 we read, "The cup of blessing which we bless, is it not a communion of the blood of Christ? The bread which we break, is it not a communion of the body of Christ?" 1 Cor. 11:27, 29 declares, "Whosoever shall eat the bread or drink the cup of the Lord in an unworthy manner, shall be guilty of the body and the blood of the Lord ... For he that eateth and drinketh, eateth and drinketh judgment unto himself, if he discern not the body." How could anyone, in receiving the sacrament, be guilty of Christ's body and blood if His body and blood are not present in the sacrament?

From the passages of Scripture just quoted we see that in the Lord's Supper we do not receive only bread and wine, but in some mysterious yet real way we receive the body and blood of our Lord. The fact of the presence of Christ's body and blood in the sacrament is clearly stated in these passages; the manner of this presence has not been revealed. We can only say, With the bread and wine we receive the body and blood of Christ, in sacramental union with the bread and wine. More than this has not been revealed. We take the language of the words of institution literally, because there is nothing to indicate or require that it should be taken figuratively. We have here the last will and testament of Christ, and in wills every effort is made to be clear and literal in order to avoid misunderstanding.

The doctrine of the real presence of the body and blood of Christ in this sacrament is stressed here, because so many have denied it. The Reformed churches teach that only bread and wine are received, and not the body and blood of Christ, as the Scriptures teach. These churches teach that the bread and wine only represent the body and blood of Christ. The bread and wine are only symbols of Christ's body and blood. But to say, as some do, that it is not possible for Christ to be really present in the sacrament, is to deny that all things are possible with God. We cannot reject the doctrine of the real presence because there is an element of mystery in it, nor because it may be beyond our comprehension. We have only to ascertain, "What saith the Scriptures?" But the Scriptures plainly declare, "This is my body," "This is my blood." We cannot explain this, but we can believe it.

The Roman Catholic church teaches that in the sacrament the bread is changed into the body of

Christ, and the wine is changed into the blood of Christ [Transubstantiation]. They hold that what is received is no longer bread and wine, but only the body and blood of Christ. But 1 Cor. 10:16 quoted above shows that the bread remains bread, and the wine remains wine. But in, with, and under these earthly elements we receive the body and blood of the risen and glorified Savior. "The cup of blessing which we bless, is it not a communion of the blood of Christ? The bread which we break, is it not a communion of the body of Christ?" The earthly elements (bread and wine) are not mixed or mingled with the body and blood of Christ to form a new substance (consubstantiation). But the body and blood of our Savior are received together with the bread and wine.

THE PURPOSE AND VALUE
OF THE LORD'S SUPPER

The Lord's Supper was instituted for us by the best Friend the world has ever had. From that fact we know that it is meant to bring us a blessing. Christ instituted this sacrament in the night in which He was betrayed. It was the last thing He did for us before He began the final struggle with His enemies. That He just then, when He knew He so soon was to suffer and die, took time to institute this Supper makes us doubly certain that it is something vital and something to help and bless us greatly.

"In the Lord's Supper we receive Christ's body and blood, which were offered up for us, as a powerful pledge of the forgiveness of sins" (S. 369). This sacrament is to give believers assurance that their sins are forgiven. "It brings believers into spiritual union with their Lord and Savior, who imparts Himself to them, and thereby preserves and strengthens them in faith, hope, and love unto eternal life" (S. 370). Here we receive gifts infinitely more precious than gold or costly jewels; here we receive the holy body and blood of the Son of God. These precious gifts we receive as tokens of God's mercy, as a pledge of His forgiveness. Thus the sacrament becomes a great comfort to troubled souls; it strengthens our faith. The Savior who bled and died for our sins on the cross gives Himself to us through this holy Supper. He speaks peace to every poor sinner who looks to Him for help. The Lord's Supper is to lift burdens for us and to strengthen the spiritual life.

Christ also said, "This do in remembrance of me." Holy Communion is to be a memorial service. Each time we receive the sacrament we are to call to vivid remembrance how Christ suffered and died for us. We should remember His agony in Gethsemane, His bloody sweat, His crown of thorns, His pierced hands and feet. We remember His great love and His willingness to die for us. This sacrament brings us face to face with the cross and reminds us of the grand central truth of the Bible, the atonement. Thus in spirit to view the Savior on the cross ever reminds us of the greatness of our sins; for ours was no small wound since it could be healed only by the pierced hands and feet and wounded brow of the Son of God (1 Peter 2:24). But it also assures us that the penalty of our sins has been paid in full. "He was wounded for our transgressions, He was bruised for our iniquities" (Isa. 53:5). He gave Himself a ransom for all.

Sweet the moments, rich the blessing,
Which before the cross we spend;
Life and health and peace possessing,
From the sinner's dying Friend.

Truly blessed is this station,
Low before His cross to lie,
While we see divine compassion
Beaming in His gracious eye.

Receiving the Lord's Supper is also a way we can testify to our faith in Christ. Each time we commune we declare in whom we believe and whom we seek to follow. "This do, as often as ye drink it, in remembrance of me. For as often as ye eat this bread, and drink the cup, ye proclaim the Lord's death till He come" (1 Cor. 11:25-26).

COMMUNION

The Lord's Supper is called Communion, for several reasons. In the first place, there is a close union between the earthly elements (bread and wine) and the body and blood of Christ. Then, this sacrament effects a closer spiritual union between the believer and Christ. Finally, God's children become more closely united with one another by thus receiving together the Lord Jesus in His sacrament. "Seeing that we, who are many, are one bread, one body: for we all partake of the one bread" (1 Cor. 10:17).

WORTHY AND UNWORTHY

The Word of God says, 1 Cor. 11:28, "Let a man prove [examine] himself, and so let him eat of the bread and drink of the cup." "Whosoever shall eat the bread or drink the cup of the Lord in an unworthy manner, shall be guilty of the body and the blood of the Lord" (1 Cor. 11:27). It is a serious thing to receive the Lord's Supper unworthily. In this sacrament we receive the most sacred gifts which God gives to men here below, the body and blood of His Son. It behooves us to make diligent and careful preparation when we are to commune. The Lord's Supper is food for God's children. It is not intended for the impenitent and unbelieving. They only eat and drink judgment unto themselves (1 Cor. 11:29).

Some go to Communion who are not worthy. Some stay away who ought to go. After all has been said about the seriousness of going to Communion, we know that it was instituted for sinners, not for angels or perfect saints. It is meant for all who confess their sins and thirst for righteousness. "The more deeply we feel our unworthiness, and the more eagerly we long for God's forgiveness, the better fitted we are to receive His grace" (S. 384). It is Christ with His comforting "Whosoever cometh unto me, I shall in no wise cast out," not Moses with his stern "Thou shalt" and "Thou shalt not," who meets the penitent sinner at the Communion table. The Lord's Supper is gospel, not law. Jesus says, "If any man thirst, let him come unto me, and drink" (John 7:37). "Blessed are they that do hunger and thirst after righteousness: for they shall be filled" (Matt. 5:6). If you long for forgiveness and for power to win the victory over sin, come. The holy sacrament is for you. Accept the body and blood of Christ as a token of God's love for you and as a pledge of forgiveness, and go on your way rejoicing.

CONFESSION AND ABSOLUTION

As a preparatory service for the Lord's Supper, we have the service of confession and absolution. "Confession embraces two parts: one that we confess our sins; the other that we receive absolution or forgiveness from the pastor as from God Himself, and in no wise doubt, but firmly believe that through it our sins are forgiven before God in heaven" (Luther's Catechism). The pastor does not forgive sins in absolution. But on God's behalf he declares to those who confess their sins that they have forgiveness. "Christ Himself has instituted absolution in order to strengthen our faith in the grace of God (Matt. 18:18; John 20:23). This power of the keys, as it is called, has been given to the church. Ordinarily the church exercises this power through the pastor whom it has called. However, in case of need, any Christian may absolve a penitent sinner. Among us confession and absolution have come to be used as a preparatory service for the Lord's Supper.

QUESTIONS

What is the Lord's Supper? Why do we believe in the real presence of Christ's body and blood in this sacrament? How does the Lutheran view of this sacrament differ from the Reformed view? How does the Lutheran view differ from the Roman Catholic view? What is the meaning of "This do in remembrance of me"? In what way does the Lord's Supper comfort us? Explain the meaning of "As often as ye eat this bread and drink this cup ye proclaim his death till he come." Why is the Lord's Supper called communion? Why is it so serious a matter to receive the Lord's Supper unworthily? Who are worthy guests at the Lord's table? Is the Lord's Supper law or gospel?

CHAPTER TEN

DUTIES IN THE CHURCH

It is God's will that His children should band themselves together in congregations, for worship, for mutual help and encouragement, and for work. Christians need one another. It is not good for them to stand alone. In all ages God has plainly shown that He desires that His people should unite in worship and work. We observe that wherever the apostle Paul labored in the Gentile world the believers came together in congregations. To these congregations he wrote most of his epistles. To such congregations God has entrusted the means of grace, the Word and the sacraments (Heb. 10:25; Matt. 18:17; Acts 2:46-47).

MEMBERSHIP

Every Christian should be a church member. Not to join a church generally leads to neglect of hearing the Word, and almost invariably to neglect of the Lord's Supper. One may contend that it is possible to be a Christian and not join any congregation. But if all should assume this attitude, there would be no congregations. No one should claim as a right for himself that which would have serious consequences if all should make the same claim.

Moreoever, affiliating with a church is also one way of showing the world on what side we stand and which side we are supporting. There is a great conflict between good and evil, between the children of light and the children of darkness, between God and the devil. No Christian should seem to be neutral. Christ says, "He that is not with me is against me" (Matt. 12:30). A Christian should be wholly on God's side and join those who are trying to do God's work.

USE OF THE MEANS OF GRACE

It is the duty of every church member to use the Word of God and the Lord's Supper diligently. To shut oneself out from the blessed power and influence of these means of grace is as disastrous to the spiritual life as to deprive oneself of food would be to the body. No one can long neglect these means of grace and remain a Christian. God's law says, "Remember the Sabbath day, to keep it holy." Luther's Catechism explains that this means that we should fear and love God and not despise preaching and His Word, but deem it holy and gladly hear and learn it. God has commanded that His Word be preached. But the command to preach is also, by inference, a command to hear. "Blessed are they that hear the Word of God, and keep it" (Luke 11:28). Sunday should be observed as *church day*. Let every Christian take heed lest by word or deed he help or encourage the movement which is threatening to sweep away Sunday as a day of worship. (Psalm 84:1-2; Heb. 10-25; Luke 11:28).

God's Word says, "Let the Word of Christ dwell in you richly" (Col. 3:16). In addition to the Sunday service, many churches also have a mid-week meeting for the study of the Word, for prayer and testimony. With the hearing of the Word should go the reading of it. "A daily Bible diet strengthens for Bible duty."

Duties to the Children

"Train up a child in the way he should go, and even when he is old he will not depart from it" (Prov. 22:6). It is the duty of parents to bring up their children in the nurture and admonition of the Lord. First of all they should bring them to God in baptism. As soon as the children are able to understand they should be told of their heavenly Father and of Jesus, the children's Friend. As they grow older they should be sent to Sunday school, confirmation class, and such other religious instruction as the church may provide. In every home there should be family worship, with prayer and the reading of some portion of the Bible. Thus young and old will be blessed together. Both by good example and by instruction we should seek to bring the children to Jesus.

Saved to Serve

With every privilege or blessing which we enjoy goes a corresponding obligation. And it is the nature of the new life that the Christian wants to help others. We are saved to serve. The deep desire of the true Christian is, "Bless me, Lord, and make me a blessing." We must not be content merely to receive. We must give ourselves in loving service for others. All are to be laborers in God's vineyard, and co-workers with God (1 Cor. 3:9). Every Christian should feel the unsaved, at home and in heathen land, a burden on his heart. He should have a passion for souls. Every Christian should be a missionary; every congregation, a missionary congregation; and every organization within the congregation should have a missionary point of view. The call to us is not only, Come and be saved, but, Come and help save the world. Christ said, "Go ye therefore, and teach all nations" (Matt. 28:19). If we cannot go, we can help send those who can go. The motive should be love for Christ and love for all those whom He loves. "The love of Christ constraineth us" (2 Cor. 5:14).

STEWARDSHIP

God has made us stewards of the talents and possessions which He has entrusted to us. All that we are and all that we have belongs to God. We speak of our money and our property, but the real owner is God. Our ownership is subject to the higher ownership of God. "The earth is the Lord's, and the fullness thereof" (1 Cor. 10:26). God does not need to beg. The silver and the gold are His, and the cattle upon a thousand hills (Haggai 2:8; Ps. 50:10). We may have a clear title to what we call ours, so far as our fellowmen are concerned. But we must acknowledge the prior right of God. In the last analysis, we are not owners at all, but stewards set to administer what God has entrusted to us so long as it pleases Him to leave us in charge. We must give account to Him of how we have administered that which is His. We are not only to be honest in earnings, but we are also to obey God in spending. God expects that a part of what He gives us shall be used to help others and to promote the work of His kingdom. To own is to owe. But many have failed to realize the importance of liberal giving. They show the worst side of their nature when approached for money. "Every man according as he purposeth in his heart, so let him give; not grudgingly, or of necessity: for God loveth a cheerful giver" (2 Cor. 9:7). God has promised a special blessing for the liberal giver (Luke 6:38; Mal. 3:7-10).

Giving should be according to one's means, as God has prospered one (1 Cor. 16:1-2). Those who have received much should give much, those who have received less should give less. The widow's mite is great in the sight of God when it is all one can give (See Mark 12:41-44). In the Old Testament time God required one-tenth. The New Testament rule for each one is: "as he may prosper" (1 Cor. 16:2).

We are not only stewards of such money and material possessions as we may have, but also of the abilities and opportunities which God gives us. The ability to sing, teach, speak, administer the business affairs of the congregation, and the like, are all talents to be used in the service of God and His church. We must not hide our talents "in a napkin of sloth and idleness." Whatever talent God may have given us, should be yielded back to Him for service.

> Let none hear you idly saying,
> "There is nothing I can do,"
> While the souls of men are dying
> And the Master calls for you.
>
> Take the task He gives you gladly,
> Let His work your pleasure be,
> Answer quickly when He calls you,
> "Here am I. Send me, send me."

SYNODS

The several local congregations band themselves together into larger organizations, usually called synods. The synod and the local congregation are mutually interdependent. Without the synod, the general work of the church, such as educating ministers and missionaries; doing mission work at home and abroad; caring for the orphaned, the aged, the unfortunate; and publishing church papers could scarcely be carried on. But without the support of the local congregations there can be no synodical work.

PRAYER FOR THE CHURCH

Jesus has taught us to pray, "Thy kingdom come." A church of praying people is an invincible force. We should pray that God may give His Word success. We should pray that the church may never lose its passion for souls. We should pray for the unity of the church, "That they may all be one." Jesus prayed for this, and all Christians should yearn for it. But the unity worth having is unity in faith, not merely in external organization. The latter without the former would have little value.

QUESTIONS

Why should a Christian join a church? What is the result of neglect of hearing the Word? What is the duty of the church to the children? What was Christ's great missionary command? What should move us to earnest missionary endeavor? Who is the real owner of the things which we possess? Why do we have synods, or general church bodies?

THE LUTHERAN CHURCH

The Lutheran Church is named after the great Reformer of the church, Martin Luther.

Luther was born in Eisleben, Germany, November 10, 1483. he was a pious young man who became first a monk and then a priest in the Roman Catholic Church. He sought with great earnestness to do according to all the teachings of his church in the hope that he might find peace for his soul and the assurance that he was just before God. He fasted much and tortured himself in various ways. The church taught that this was especially pleasing in the sight of God. But these things gave him no peace or assurance. But at last he saw a new light. "The just shall live *by faith*" (Rom. 1:17; Gal. 3:11). It is not by our merit we are saved, but by the merits of Jesus Christ. All that Jesus did for us becomes ours when we believe in Him. We are justified by faith, not by works. When this dawned on Luther, his troubled soul found peace and he was a happy man.

When Luther now continued the study of the Word of God he saw the Roman church had departed from the teaching of the Bible on many points. Just at this time the church was selling indulgences. For money the church offered to sell the forgiveness of sins, either for a specified period or for life, according to the amount paid. In theory, the indulgences were to be given to those who were penitent. The payment of money was to be an evidence of repentance. But in practice, little was said about repentance if the money was forthcoming.

Luther could hold his peace no longer. October 31, 1517, he nailed a document, known in history as the Ninety-Five Theses, upon the door of the castle church at Wittenberg. In the Ninety-five Theses he clearly showed the false teachings of the church of Rome. This document made a tremendous impression. Many believed and felt as Luther did. Thus began the great Protestant Reformation.

At first Luther and his followers did not intend to leave the Roman church. They wanted only to cleanse the church of its false teachings and practices. It taught that tradition and the decrees of popes and church councils had the same authority as the Bible. It taught that we become just before God, not by faith in Christ alone and through grace alone, but by faith and works of merit which man must do. It taught that prayers should be made to the saints, especially to Virgin Mary, and not to the triune God alone. The church had the doctrine of purgatory, which is found nowhere in the Bible, and the doctrine of the surplus merits of the saints. These and other corruptions in the teachings of the church, Luther and his followers pointed out. They hoped that the church might be cleansed.

The answer of the church was the excommunication of Luther and denunciation of all his followers. At the Diet of Worms, April, 1521, Luther was commanded to retract. His answer was, "Unless I am convinced by Scripture or other clear proofs, I neither can nor dare retract anything, for my conscience is bound in God's Word. Here I stand; I cannot do otherwise; so help me God, Amen."

It was not very long before there came to be divisions among the Protestants. Differences in interpretation of the Scriptures developed, especially in the matter of the sacraments. Those who agreed with Luther's interpretations came to be called Lutherans. (This name was first used by the enemies of Luther.) The other Protestants have come to bear the general name, Reformed. Among the Reformed there are various denominations, such as Presbyterian, Baptist, Congregational, Episcopal, and Methodist Episcopal.

The confessions (symbols) formulated in the earliest centuries of the Christian Church are the Apostles' Creed, the Nicene Creed, and the Athanasian Creed. The Lutheran Church holds these confessions in common with various other Christian denominations. The specifically Lutheran confessions are the Augsburg Confession and Luther's Catechism. All the confessional documents of the Lutheran Church are found in a volume called *The Book of Concord.*

The Lutheran Church is the largest Protestant church in the world, having about 84,000,000 members. It is third in size in the United States, with 3,103,456 confirmed members (1936). The Lutherans first came to America in 1628. Partly because of the various nationalities, and hence the different languages used, Lutherans were divided into several groups or synods. These synods differ mainly in their forms of service and practice, but all have adopted the Augsburg Confession and Luther's Catechism as their confessions.

In doctrine the Lutheran Church of America is conservative. It desires to cling tenaciously to the faith once delivered to the saints. Its slogan is: "The Word alone, grace alone, faith alone." It does not want to be "wise above what is written." It takes the open Bible as its guide. It proclaims a divine Savior, the Son of God, whose blood shed for us on the cross atoned for all sin. It believes that by our own strength we cannot come to Christ or believe in Him, but the Holy Spirit, by the means of grace, gives us the faith in Christ through which we are accounted righteous in the sight of God. The fruit of this faith must be a holy life, after the pattern of Christ Himself.